See Dick and Jane Grow Up

Seven Growth Steps to Marital Maturity

Dr. David B. Hawkins

Love. Honor. Cherish.
faithmarriage.com

Faith Marriage is an imprint of
Cook Communications Ministries, Colorado Springs, Colorado 80918
Cook Communications, Paris, Ontario
Kingsway Communications, Eastbourne, England

Printed in the United States of America.

1 2 3 4 5 6 7 8 9 10 Printing/Year 05 04 03 02 01

Editor: Greg Clouse, Janet Lee
Cover Design: Lovgren Advertising
Interior Design: RJS Design

Acknowledgments

When I think of the origins and preparation of this book, I am thankful to a number of people who helped it through the birth process. The initial ideas for the book occurred in an unlikely place—a poolside in Acapulco. I must thank my wife, Diane, and my sister-in-law, Judy, for their zany and creative banter that spawned the ideas that led to this book. Keep it up girls!

While the original ideas were ours together, I am ultimately responsible for the final product. Many people, however, have come alongside me and helped give it a form and structure that is so much more readable.

First, let me thank Greg Clouse, my editor at ChariotVictor, who has believed in my work for several years. Greg, your support, and that of the staff at ChariotVictor, is so encouraging to me. Go Broncos!

Second, Lee Hough must be recognized. He and Greg invited me down to Colorado Springs to draw diagrams and flow charts on a blackboard all day to see how this book should be structured. Again, my raw ideas were transformed, sometimes painfully, by their gentle, creative brainstorming. I really was paying attention, Lee.

In the middle of the process my friend Judith Irwin was a caretaker of the manuscript. As a writer/ teacher she taught me more about "show, don't tell." More importantly she taught me to speak from the heart. "I can always tell when you are sharing your heart, or just talking to people," she would kindly counsel. Thanks, Judith.

Then Gary Wilde entered the picture. He added yet another layer of finesse to the manuscript. You can thank him for many of the extras you will find in this book. Thanks for your creative genius Gary.

Finally, I must thank my wonderful wife Diane for all the hours she spent either driving (while I whittled away on the manuscript with my trusty laptop) or being abandoned while I worked in my office. But she always encourages my writing, for which I am grateful. I also thank her for her patience as I try to live out the principles in this book. For twenty-seven years she has, in many ways and settings, encouraged me to practice what I preach. Many of the lessons in this book have come directly from our marriage experience; we still need them and we still use them.

I love you, Diane.

—David B. Hawkins, Ph.D.
Spring, 2001

Contents

Introduction:
Time to Grow Up!

Dick.
Jane.
See Dick and Jane.
Come here and look. . . .

Do you remember these young children? Actually, they're physically grown now, but they were young once, like you and me. They were thrilled and excited to explore their world. Everything was new and fun. Even when trouble appeared, as it undoubtedly did, it was still an adventure to meet it. We traveled with them on their adventures, and our worlds became larger because of them.

Dick and Jane passed through elementary school without too many scrapes and bruises. They had fun exploring their world. They had big plans for the future. Some of their plans worked out; many did not.

They went on to attend college and find meaningful employment. Both Dick and Jane married their high school sweethearts and planned for everything to have a storybook ending. And why not? They'd been taught to believe that, if they lived right, everything would fall into place. But it didn't happen that way.

They got married to their partners . . . and their problems began.

See Dick and Jane shout.
See Jane stomp away in anger.
See Dick pout.
See Dick and Jane clam up.

And so the story goes—their story, and ours as well. Dick and Jane had to learn from their difficulties how to keep a marriage healthy. A good marriage does not just happen. It's a challenge; it takes effort and struggle.

Your Challenge Too?

Yes, we too are called to leave our world of childlike fantasies for the real world of adulthood and responsibility. But many of us, unfortunately, refuse to leave the Dick-and-Jane world behind. We've grown up physically but not emotionally. Still playing our childish games, we insist on our own way and wonder why our marriages aren't happy.

You see, if, instead of taking responsibility for our own feelings, we get angry and regress into the comfort of two-year-old mentalities, we tend to—

- restrict our vision, thus blinding us to creative solutions;
- overreact, letting our emotions have too much control;
- see things in terms of extremes, thus amplifying the problem;
- generate adrenaline, leading to a fight-or-flight response;
- plant our feet, thereby resisting compromises.

Many of these behaviors are remnants of attitudes we had as children. That is why we're not far off when we shout, "Grow up!" to one another. Knowing what ways of thinking and behaving are childish, and learning some options for giving them up, will help us create the safe, zestful, passionate marriages we are all seeking.

That is my hope for you and your marriage.

This book is for those of us who need to let go of childish wishes and behaviors that hamper adult relationships. The problem is, these attitudes are subtle enough to keep us confused. So often we don't even recognize what's happening within us to cause such relational anguish in the marriage. Nevertheless, you no doubt recognize that it will take a radical change on the inside for you to find satisfaction in your marriage. You may be preparing yourself for this deep level of change and are looking for the tools to help you accomplish it.

You have come to the right place! While I won't offer magical, childlike answers, I'll clearly demonstrate: *there are answers*. There are tried-and-true principles for growing up and facing marital challenges. Let's briefly look at the some of the key principles we'll be exploring . . .

First, we will look at the twin tasks of choosing to change and of learning from our mistakes. Because we're creatures of habit, and because we tend to keep doing what we have always done, we lead lives of disappointment. Our childhood patterns will not work in our adult worlds.

We will also learn how to broaden our perspectives so that we aren't simply preoccupied with meeting our own needs while failing to acknowledge our spouse's needs. Pure self-centeredness has no place in our adult world.

Our manual for adult married living also explores the requirement of good, effective communication. We'll learn that active listening is another form of giving to our spouses. At best we're often listening out of polite obligation as a price to pay for our own turn to speak. This childish pattern defeats the very intimacy we yearn for most.

Part of growing up means lessening our grip on things we consider to be "ours." While we all know that we need to learn to share, it's hard for most of us to do. We may have gotten away with hogging the toys when we were seven years old, but today selfishness truly disrupts our relationships and causes distrust and resentment.

One of the most important chapters of the book explores how to "own our stuff." Blaming one another is a common game occurring in most marriages. It takes self-confidence and maturity to face our foibles and work on them. Little else can help a marriage as much as taking responsibility for our mistakes.

Our book will review the important art of keeping the marital slate clear of grudges. Saying, "I'm sorry," and practicing forgiveness, remain two of our most difficult lessons. Like Dick and Jane, the child in each of us resists granting a pardon to those we resent.

Finally, we'll get quite practical about adding adventure and enjoyment to a marriage. It is so easy to let the mundane routines of life crowd out our need for excitement. The kid in us still craves play, and we will either find constructive or destructive ways to experience the joy that comes with "fun."

How Are the Chapters Organized?

You will uncover plenty of information in each of the chapters to come. I'll draw on my years of experience as a clinical psychologist and marriage counselor to explore issues and illustrate with name-changed case studies. You'll also find interesting sidebars and exercises drawn from the work of others to help you put your learning into practice, day by day.

I want this book to do more than inform you—I also want it to draw you into the actual process of change. To that end, each chapter concludes with a MARRIAGE MAKEOVER PLAN. These plans will move you and your spouse, step by step, through the seven growth steps to marital maturity. I challenge you to promise one another at the outset of your reading to move through these Makeover Plans together. You may wish to take several weeks doing it, perhaps reading a chapter per week. Naturally, the process can't be rushed. But if you will both commit to the sharing, discussing, brainstorming—and *doing*—in these Plans, I know you'll radically improve your marriage.

In each chapter you'll be following an ongoing storyline of "Dick and Linda," and "Jane and Rob." You'll observe their everyday conversations—the high points and the low points. Most importantly, you will observe what happens when immaturity creeps into mature relationships. That's why each of the Marriage Makeover Plans offers the opportunity to work on one specific way of growing up. In quick review, here are the seven growth steps and tasks for renewing love and commitment in your marriage:

Step #1: Moving from Discouragement to Possibility
Key task: *While learning from the past, make a solid, mutual commitment to change.*

Step #2: Moving from "Me" to "We"
Key task: *Determine to treat your spouse as a beloved partner rather than a live-in competitor.*

Step #3: Moving from Blame to Responsibility
Key task: *Learn the reasons for, and methods of, unfair attacking—and avoid them at all costs.*

Step #4: Moving from Taking to Giving
Key task: *Look deep within yourself to confront "emptiness" and codependent patterns of relating.*

Step #5: Moving from Silence to Sharing
Key task: *Confront the unhealthy silence within you, while learning and practicing good communication skills.*

Step #6: Moving from Grudges to Forgiveness
Key task: *Seek forgiveness—from yourself and your spouse—then offer it liberally.*

Step #7: Moving from Apathy to Adventure
Key task: *Together, walk through the six steps to restoring marital adventure.*

Ready for a Transformed Marriage?

The whole theme of this book is that we have problems in our marriages because in certain areas *we just haven't grown up yet!* But are you ready to grow up?

I had to come to that point myself. Several years ago, my wife and I attended a marriage workshop that included some things I'd never heard in my years of training. You see, so much of what I read and hear involves "fixing" problem areas in a marriage. I must confess that I too have often narrowed my approach to counseling from that perspective. But the couple leading this workshop helped us to see how marriage can be a place where we *work in tandem with God to grow into the kinds of people we were designed to be.* This is a thoroughly positive, pro-active task. A marriage is an exciting workshop, so to speak, where the rough edges are smoothed, sometimes with difficulty, but always with the potential for tremendous growth.

This perspective challenged me to quit complaining that my wife didn't always see the world the way I did—or the way I *expected* her to see it. I've since learned to appreciate more fully her unique personality, her strengths and weaknesses . . . and be thankful for them. This new point of view helped me to be alert for how she could enhance my strengths and confront my weaknesses, as well. We've grown up a bit because of it. And it feels good.

Can you relate? Most couples who've been married for any length of time have not only faced conflicts *within* their marriage, but they have also weathered the challenges that originate *outside* of the relationship. For example, couples must work together to weather the loss of a long-standing job. They must communicate about how they will navigate a major illness or accident. Even the normal progression leading to an eventual "empty nest" can inflict havoc on entrenched family rituals. How do couples adapt to such changes? Hopefully, they will see them as opportunities to change and grow rather than as disasters leading to unwanted setbacks and stagnation.

I believe all of us have the opportunity in our marriages to perform acts of kindness at crucial times, showing sensitivity that will help our spouses grow in strength of character. We can minister by acknowledging our partner's troublesome struggles and care enough to offer encouragement. We can assist in creating an environment around the home that provides a shelter from the storms of life. The home, if both work on it, can be a wonderful place to be after facing the trials of the day.

Someone has said that life happens when we are making other plans. I think the same can be said for marriage. It happens in the little nooks and crannies of daily routines. Each day can be a building block to strengthen the foundation of your marriage. Or it can be a brick, part of a wall which can separate you from your spouse forever. Therefore I encourage you to use every opportunity to nurture your relationship with your spouse. I hope this book will help you do it.

Finally, be assured that a dynamic marriage is possible. Using the growth steps and tasks outlined in this book, you can continue to grow and challenge yourselves to new, healthier ways of interacting. These tools can keep your marriage from becoming stagnant. While you'll encounter many disappointments, even these can be building blocks to marital intimacy. So follow me as we have some fun exploring our old, childish ways of interacting. It's time to give them up in favor of making your marriage the blissful experience it was always meant to be.

—David B. Hawkins, Ph.D.
June 2001

Part 1 The Problem

(See Dick and Jane . . . Hurting!)

1 Needing to Change

H elp, Dick! Help with the work!
See Dick run.
Run, Dick! Run fast!

Dick and Jane were delightful children. A quick review of the elementary school primers shows them giggling and laughing their way through life. Every day was an adventure, and we lived out our own lives vicariously through their escapades. They were adorable, naturally playful, spontaneous, and a bit mischievous.

However, children are not *just* playful and adorable. They are also naturally irresponsible and demanding. They are unbelievably self-centered. And they typically think only of their own needs and desires.

All Grown Up?

Yet children do grow up—at least physically—while often bringing many of the unpleasant traits of childishness along with them into adulthood. This caused problems for Dick and his new wife, Linda. . . .

Dick and Linda: Running a Household?

When Dick "grew up" he married Linda, and things were fine for the first couple of years. When I say "fine," I mean they tolerated certain problems and conflicts common to any couple trying to merge two separate and strong wills. They faced issues like deciding who would clean up the kitchen after a meal, who would take out the garbage every morning, and who would keep the car gassed and oiled. For them, the everyday challenge of balancing work and play, while running a household, became a persistent source of contention.

Linda was attending college when they married, and Dick worked for a landscaping firm. He worked long hours, and when he was "off," he wanted to play. This unspoken agreement—that Dick could play while Linda studied—didn't take into account that certain household chores would keep demanding their attention.

Exhausted by her part-time job, her studies, and her never-ending work around the house, Linda's attitude toward Dick's "play" gradually began to change. She repeatedly asked for his help with the chores so she could focus more on her school homework. But Dick had other things on his mind, such as four-wheeling, skiing, and biking. It wasn't that he was against helping her around the house; he just seemed to have a higher tolerance for "mess." A few dirty towels laying on the floor, or a stack of newspapers gathering dust in the corner, didn't bother him in the least. *Why is she so uptight about this stuff?* he wondered.

Linda soon tired of reminding her husband to pick up after himself. The gentle teasing gave way to nagging, which ended in screaming. Dick resented Linda's "explosive temper" and labeled her a perfectionist. He felt she overreacted to the "little messes" around the house.

The tiny relational rift soon grew into a Grand Canyon of animosity. Both sulked and harbored grudges. She resented having to treat him like a child. He railed against her constant "mothering." Caught in a vicious spiral of defensiveness ("Not me, but *you* are to blame"), and failing to recognize the unique aspects of childishness they each poured into the fight, they faced an ever-widening chasm of hurt.

Rob and Jane: Fighting about Finances

Jane fared little better than Dick in her marriage. In her early twenties she had married Rob, a pharmaceutical representative, and she worked in the sales department of a local clothing store. Rob had been attracted to Jane and her "cute obsession" with looking good. She liked nothing more than spending the weekend shopping for clothes. Indeed, she had a knack for finding just the right outfit to enhance her appearance.

Rob at first thought Jane's little fixation on eye-appealing clothes was charming. He even got a special thrill from seeing how other men envied him. But the hours and hours Jane spent in the super-malls began to annoy him. For a time they joked about this growing area of contention. Rob didn't know how to address the issue directly and was afraid of conflict. Jane didn't want to budget or keep track of her spending. But the overspending wasn't just limited to clothes. In time, with bank overdrafts and escalating credit debt piling up, Rob concluded that Jane had a serious spending problem.

When he tried to talk about "their problem," Jane became defensive. After all, she needed fine clothes in her career. His every effort to get an agreement from her was met with a similar rationalization. In short, Jane just didn't want to hear what Rob had to say.

More conservative in his spending, Rob had set his sights on owning a home and creating a secure financial future. Although they earned excellent incomes, achieving long-term financial goals would depend on disciplined adherence to a planned budget. Verbally, Jane agreed to all of this. Yet her weekend spending sprees continued, and she became irritated with Rob when he brought up the subject. *Doesn't he love me more than money?* In her mind it was so simple:

See Rob love Jane.
Love, Rob, love!
Love me just the way I am.

Jane felt Rob was demanding that she turn into some abstract idea of his, a far-off vision of "their future." Constant money fights lowered the temperature on their relationship until they labored under a layered iceberg of resentments. Would they survive the cold?

*****

Dick and Jane's kind of troubles transcend the boundaries of time and culture; their basic issues are universal. In the Bible, the Apostle Paul knew about the destructive effects of childishness in adults; in fact, he continually challenged Christians to "grow up." For example, he addressed the Corinthian believers as "mere infants in Christ" who were "worldly" and not spiritual, and chided them for their quarreling and jealous rangling (see 1 Corinthians 3). His description of their conflicts sounds similar to those unfolding in many homes today. Whether in church or at home, whether then or now, childish behavior in an adult is rarely cute.

But in order to change, we adults must make a firm and well-considered *choice*.

Why is that so difficult? Perhaps it's because we aren't fully aware of (1) the serious obstacles to change and (2) what change will immediately require of us.

The Obstacles to Change

It's said that long ago a king set up a test for his subjects. He placed a boulder on a roadway and then hid himself to see if anyone would remove the troublesome obstacle. Some of the king's wealthiest merchants and courtiers came by and simply walked around the huge rock. Many loudly blamed the king for not keeping the roads clear, but none did anything about moving the stone away.

Then a peasant came along carrying a load of vegetables. Upon approaching the boulder, he laid down his burden and tried to move the stone to the side of the road. After much pushing and straining, he finally succeeded—and then noticed a purse lying in the road where the boulder had been.

Gold coins!

And along with the coins, a note from the king: anyone who removed the boulder could keep the gold. The peasant learned what many others never understand: *Every obstacle presents an opportunity to improve one's condition.* Often, however, we are hurtling down the pathways of life too frantically. We rarely stop to listen for the message meant for us in every potentially maddening roadblock and irritating detour. What, specifically, are these impediments? Let's look briefly at some of the more common obstacles to changing course, even when we know we're headed for a marital dead end.

• *Remaining stuck in patterned behaviors.* We bring the past into our marriages. We bring with us all of the various patterns of relating that we learned from growing up with Mom and Dad: the way we were encouraged (or not), disciplined, complimented, nurtured, and comforted. All of these patterns, which became firmly ingrained aspects of our "relational repertoire," we bring with us into the marriage.

So we might say that, in different ways, both Dick and Jane were living out their sandbox immaturities, the ingrained childish behaviors that now wreak havoc in adulthood. They are stuck, and if they refuse to deal directly with these patterned behaviors, they will remain stranded on the highway to a happy home.

Can you see where Dick and Jane need to "grow up"? For example, what if these two adults had been trained in more self-discipline when they were kids? Suppose that Jane's childhood pouting and whining (when she wanted a cute but costly outfit) had not worked quite so often? Suppose she'd learned to shop for bargains, save her money, and delay her gratification?

Suppose Dick had learned to put away his toys, straighten up his room, hang up his clothes? And, later, what if he had learned that coming in from the ball field or back from a skiing trip, he ought to be ready to do his own laundry, perhaps fix the dinner, or at least wash the dishes?

In other words, Dick and Jane are living out of old habit molds and failing to learn from them. They're practicing some patterns that could prove fatal to their marriages if they do not change.

• *Denying painful reality.* It's no secret that some of us choose to live the life of a victim. In a sense, we opt for wearing the proverbial sign on our backs—"Kick Me!" Denying our own role in creating so much of our pain, we can even begin feeling sorry for ourselves. But denying what "is" only compounds the problem; we must have an accurate diagnosis before we can move on to a cure.

It's easier to avoid the diagnosis, however. Some friends of ours in the Old Testament—Adam and Eve—modeled a pattern of behavior that many of us use to this day. When confronted with the fact of their sinful behavior, they used the tactic of hiding. Then they hurled accusations and blame at each other. I believe it's guilt that causes us to hide and hurl. We dare not sit in one place to let the light of truth shine on us, because that can be such a frightening experience. It takes courage and faith to grow up and face the painful truths of our lives.

> # Danger Here!
> ### Messages about Feelings
>
> Children receive a great many messages about feelings—what feelings are okay to have, what feelings are okay to express, and what feelings are not okay to have or to express. Here are some of the more common messages about feelings that children receive either directly or indirectly. Check off the ones that apply to you—
>
> ____ Don't be scared. Don't say what you feel.
> ____ Be scared. Life's depressing.
> ____ Life's scary. You're just a pouter.
> ____ You're a crybaby. You have a chip on your shoulder.
> ____ Big boys don't cry. Laughter makes the world go around.
> ____ Don't be a sissy. Enjoy life!
> ____ You're always angry about something.
> ____ Keep smiling!
> ____ We don't get angry in this family. You have a great laugh.[1]

The truth of the matter is that we are all guilty of wrongdoing. We live in a fallen world and are limited. Our limits express themselves as mistakes, faults, inappropriate behaviors, and simple foolish choices. Yet our only shame is trying to deny, hide, or run from these problems rather than face them with childlike simplicity and openness. As we honestly face our problems—amidst the painful reality that we ourselves have usually created them!—we can then ask for the

Technical Talk

How might a psychologist describe the childishness in Dick and Jane? Consider what the two are doing:

- They escape into denial.
(**"I don't need to change."**)
- They pursue blame-shifting. (**"You have the problem, not me."**)
- They use avoidance as a "flight response." (**"Just leave me alone."**)
- They attempt to minimize and rationalize. (**"It's not as bad as you think."**)
- They strengthen their entrenchment. (**"I have no intention of changing."**)

help we need to change course. And, of course, our faith in Jesus assures us of a cleansed heart:

Therefore, brothers, since we have confidence to enter the Most Holy Place by the blood of Jesus, by a new and living way opened for us through the curtain, that is, his body, and since we have a great priest over the house of God, let us draw near to God with a sincere heart in full assurance of faith, having our hearts sprinkled to cleanse us from a guilty conscience and having our bodies washed with pure water. —Hebrews 10:19-22

• *Clinging to the "comfortable."* Consider this popular definition of insanity: "Doing the same thing, over and over, while expecting different results." Certainly we all can review our lives and see where we have clung to old, unworkable ways as if hoping, magically, there will be different outcomes. It's just easier that way. We've grown accustomed to doing things in certain ways in our marriages, and the effort to change seems unwarranted and hardly worth the effort.

Have you ever observed an elderly couple who have lived this way for most of their married lives? You've no doubt noticed how you can predict virtually every response in one of their "standard" arguments. The same old points and counterpoints have flown back and forth so often that these folks can conduct their little recurring spats while on intellectual and emotional autopilot. Inertia sets in—along with a loss of relational intimacy, the very thing that makes any marriage worthwhile. So why change?

Though it seems more comfortable not to attempt change, the rewards of growth-producing change are awesome. For one thing, we experience the exquisite sense of freedom that comes with the new options that invariably open up to us. When we're fully engaged with reality, life becomes a wonderland of opportunities. We become a Picasso, with the whole world as our creative canvas.

The Requirements for Change

"What will it take for you to change?" I ask my clients. Curiously, some couples ask that I help them change but seem unwilling to make a genuine effort.

In fact, I've found that we often want to feel better without attempting to change. If cornered, we will make a few cosmetic changes, but these are destined to fail. They do not last because our hearts have not truly been transformed.

This seemed to be the case with Jacob, a middle-aged man who came to my office, at the insistence of his wife, because he'd had an affair with another woman. While Jacob wanted an end to his wife's "badgering and questions," he refused to change his attitude toward what he had done. The idea of asking for forgiveness seemed out of the question. "And besides, the affair ended months ago," he said. "I shouldn't have to live on a leash forever."

Jacob's pride was quite evident, as was his lack of caring for his wife's deep hurt. She needed reassurance and healing; he needed to demonstrate a willing-

Escaping the Pain?

While our marriages cry out for honesty and intimacy, most of us are so busy posturing that we forget what is really happening inside. Dr. Dean Ornish studies the impact of stress on our cardiovascular system. He concludes: "The real epidemic in our culture is not only physical heart disease, but also what I call emotional and spiritual heart disease—that is, the profound feelings of loneliness, isolation, alienation, and depression that are so prevalent in our culture with the breakdown of social structures that used to provide us with a sense of connection and community."

Dr. Ornish goes on to share how pain in a relationship *can be very beneficial*. After our attempts at denial have faltered, we may be more motivated to look for lasting inner change.[2]

ness to explore his own raw pain—the loneliness and emptiness that had contributed to his vulnerability to a sexual affair. Yet Jacob remained unwilling to open up—how scary for him!—and reveal to his wife the true longings of his heart. Afraid of the intense emotion that would bubble to the surface, he chose not to work at "affair-proofing" his marriage. He hardened his heart and subtly, but clearly, put most of the responsibility for change on his wife's shoulders.

Jacob's story provides an excellent starting point for us as we review what change will require of us. It always demands a certain amount of discomfort in the present while holding out the prospect of a deeper happiness in the future. Specifically, change asks at least three things of us:

• *Change Requirement #1: Begin to "own your own stuff."* In other words, we must take personal responsibility for the circumstances we create and for our

Strategy Steps

Confront Those Obstacles!

The first step in confronting obstacles to change is to ask yourself some searching questions. Why not start with these:

1. What is my current problem?

2. How can I shift my point of view to see (or hear) what this is trying to teach me?

3. Is there a gift (a "gold coin" of learning or growing) hidden here somewhere? What are my clues?

4. Have I brought this matter before the Lord? What is He saying to me these days?

response to them. Consider a man who walks down the road and falls into a pothole. Cursing, he blames his pain and mournful condition on everyone around him. The next day he walks down the same road and again falls into the same pothole. Again he curses others because of his plight. The next day he walks down the same road and falls into the same hole. This time, however, he considers that he may have other options—and takes *response-ability* for his situation.

The next day he walks down a different road.

You might say this man could have avoided the pothole by simply walking around it. However, with most habitual patterns of failure, a cycle is set in motion as soon as our mind begins down the old, familiar road. Once begun, the spiral of desire inevitably leads to its conclusion, regardless of our attempts at resistance by sheer willpower. In other words, once we get on the road to our familiar failure, we're likely to travel it to the very end. People caught in any form of addiction know this to be true. And willpower alone only strengthens the habit, once we allow ourselves the first step onto the road. The solution is never to step onto that road in the first place—not even in our thoughts. And the point is: *We ourselves are responsible for staying out of our own "favorite" potholes!* This is what I mean by owning your own stuff.

I'm simply saying that if you keep having the same old problem or issue, and you keep cursing the wind, moon, sun, and anyone who might be nearby, you are probably standing in a pothole. There's no need for alarm. Think of it as a wake-up call. Avoid personal pain and embarrassment later by being perceptive now. Take personal responsibility for your own problems. Begin the change.

• *Change Requirement #2: Put on the cloak of "courageous humility."* Because change is so difficult, it requires large doses of humility so that we can face the truth. But humility is a commodity hard to come by these days because it takes real courage to look ourselves honestly in the mirror—to acknowledge destructive patterns of living and thinking. "Half measures avail us nothing," warns the Alcoholics Anonymous manual. Telling ourselves half-truths will only yield milk-toast changes.

Brennan Manning, in his wonderful book *The Ragamuffin Gospel*, illustrates the issue of half-truths by describing his experience at an alcohol rehabilitation center in a small town north of Minneapolis. His group therapy was orchestrated by a dominant man, Sean Murphy O'Connor, who had no tolerance for dishonesty, no matter how small.

One day, Mr. O'Connor began bombarding a man named Max for the truth about his drinking history. The man denied his problem, and continued to minimize the effects of his drinking in an attempt to look good in front of the other group members. Finally, Mr. O'Connor brings in a phone and calls Max's wife. He asks her whether Max has ever been unkind during his drinking days.

> ## Self-Check
>
> A "pothole" is any repeated pattern of behavior that has continually landed you in trouble or made you unhappy with yourself, your mate, or others. Think about a pothole in your own life for a moment, and ask yourself:
>
> • What potholes can I own up to?
>
> • What are the initial thinking processes that tend to put me on a bumpy road?
>
> • What options—alternative "roads"—are available to me?
>
> • What new thought patterns could I try, in order to keep the spiraling cycle of habit from kicking in?

"Yes," his wife says slowly. Then she tells of a time when Max proudly gave his young daughter sixty dollars to buy a special pair of shoes for the winter. Max decided to celebrate the occasion by stopping in at the Cork 'n' Bottle, leaving his daughter in the car because he'd "be right out."

"My husband met some old Army buddies in the tavern. Swept up in the euphoria over the reunion, he lost track of time, purpose, and everything else. He came out of the Cork 'n' Bottle at midnight. He was drunk. The motor had stopped running and the car windows were frozen shut. Debbie was badly frost-bitten on both ears and on her fingers. When we got her to the hospital, the doctors amputated the thumb and forefinger on her right hand. And she will be deaf for the rest of her life."

Max could no longer maintain the lie. He collapsed to the floor sobbing. He was now vulnerable, humbled, open to healing, forgiveness, and heart change. It took courage for him to come to that blessed place; after all, he could have stormed out of the room and continued running from his problems.

Self-Check

Steps to Acceptance

Most couples go through stages in their marriage before they reach the point of acceptance, where each loves a real person, though an admittedly imperfect person. Where do you see yourself?

Romantic Stage— "You're certainly not perfect. I'll change if you will."

Coercive Stage— "Like it or not, I'm going to change you! And if I need help, I'll sic God on you."

Desperation Stage— "You'll never change. I give up on you. I give up on our marriage (either physically or emotionally)."

Acceptance Stage— "Frankly, both of us are a bit strange. Neither of us is perfect—but I'm committed to you."[3]

True change requires humility and brokenness. Remember the comforting spiritual paradox that "in our weakness, He is made strong." The Apostle Paul (in Romans 8:26) assures us that the Holy Spirit helps us in our weakness, interceding on our behalf to the Father.

• *Change Requirement #3: Fight the familiar misery.* Rather than approaching their problems with a courageous humility, many people will settle for a predictable level of emotional misery. They opt for pain and circumstances that are, at least, familiar, and doom themselves to a suffering that will only grow worse. In such cases, the idea of perseverance becomes a major hurdle for those who expect a quick sprint. The pursuit of maturity is a race won by marathoners, not sprinters, according to psychologist Dr. Chris Thurman.[4] Alluding to the fable of the hare and the tortoise, he notes that the trail is strewn with the carcasses of rabbits who have given 110 percent . . . for a short time.

The highest hurdle is the illusion that power (and pride) will win the day. He observes that "personal power, as much as it gets held in high esteem in our culture, isn't enough to bring about deep, lasting change." The true source of power for transforming change, he says, is God—if we cooperate and "go along with his program." God will help us to change if we are willing to face the pain of changing, persevere in our struggle, and seek Him for the source of power.

In the poetry of Psalm 51, King David expresses from personal experience the transforming power of God's love in the human heart:

I *know my transgressions,*
and my sin is always before me.
Against you, you only, have I sinned
and done what is evil in your sight,
so that you are proved right when you
speak
and justified when you judge.
Surely I was sinful at birth,
sinful from the time my mother con-
ceived me.
Surely you desire truth in the inner
parts;
you teach me wisdom in the inmost
place.
Cleanse me with hyssop, and I will be
clean;
wash me, and I will be whiter than
snow.
—*Psalm 51:3-7*

See Dick and Jane Grow Up

Now let's return to the scenarios that opened this chapter. Dick and Jane are in conflict with their spouses. But suppose they were to take the first steps toward positive change? What could that look like? In other words, let's see what can happen when bro-kenness replaces pride, when possibili-ty triumphs over discouragement.

Imagine a Heart-Change in Dick . . .

One day Linda sat down with Dick, the tears welling up in her eyes. She announced that she could no longer live the way they had been living. She was frazzled with working part-time and continuing on with her studies. She felt deeply disrespected by Dick because of his consistent selfishness in his own pursuits. She used "I" statements to share how she was feeling while avoid-

---

Strategy Steps
Begin Your Spiritual Reconnection

Here's a first step for couples who want to renew their relationship: set up regular times of praying together about conflict issues—every day. As a part of your time together, commit to memorizing key, pertinent Scriptures, such as Ephesians 4:29-32—

Do not let any unwholesome talk come out of your mouths, but only what is helpful for building others up according to their needs, that it may benefit those who listen. And do not grieve the Holy Spirit of God, with whom you were sealed for the day of redemption. Get rid of all bitterness, rage and anger, brawling and slander, along with every form of malice. Be kind and compassionate to one another, forgiving each other, just as in Christ God forgave you.

Other Scriptures to check out together:

- Genesis 2:18-25
- Proverbs 5:18-20
- Proverbs 31:10-29
- Song of Songs 4:1-6; 5:10-16
- 1 Corinthians 7:1-17
- Ephesians 5:21-33
- Hebrews 13:4a
- 1 Peter 3:1-7

ing any direct accusations. This was simply a time for Linda to reveal her heart with as much transparency as she had the courage to risk.

"I don't know how else to tell you how hurt I am, Dick," Linda said. "I'm so tired of taking care of everything in our home, plus working and studying. I feel as if I'm close to a nervous breakdown."

Dick stared at her for a moment, considering what she was saying. She wasn't nagging, yelling, criticizing. She had an intensity in her voice he hadn't heard before. She was baring her soul. He reflected momentarily on the many years he had spent with her, and he knew he couldn't stand to lose this one he loved so dearly.

"Linda," Dick said, now looking at the floor. "You don't need to say anything more. I feel terrible. Actually, I've been listening to Pastor talk about sacrificial love and I've felt convicted for a long time now. You're just repeating what my heart has been saying to me for the past several months. I know I need to change. Can you be a little patient with me as I work on changing?"

Linda was silent for a moment. "Of course, if you really mean it. If you are really going to change this time."

"You have no reason to trust me, and I have doubts in my own abilities. But I do know that God is calling me to be a loving husband, and with His help I can do it."

"I sense that you are serious about this. And Lord knows, I have my own part to play in changing; I haven't been perfect, either. . . ."

See Dick.

See Dick listen.

Listen, Dick. Listen now!

Imagine a Heart-Change in Jane . . .

Rob sat down one evening with Jane, even though he feared that she would lash out at the messenger, once again, for bringing an unwanted message. He had prayed about this encounter ahead of time, hoping beyond hope that it would go well.

"Jane, I want to talk about money again. I feel a real burden about this, even though I hate dealing with it as much as you do," he said.

"I kind of doubt that," Jane retorted sarcastically.

"Well, I can assure you that I don't like to talk about it. And I definitely don't want to fight. I mean, I've probably never really shared with you how much it hurts me inside when we yell at each other. I feel so sad when we say mean things.

. . . I love you so much."

Jane took a moment to consider Rob's words. They seemed to be coming straight from his heart, filled with genuine concern. And she'd known all along that this conversation had to take place. In fact, she knew that it was long overdue and Rob's nonaccusing tone helped her to lower her defenses and open up.

"It's okay to talk about it. I've been thinking about it too, and I know that I have to face some things." Of course, Jane partially wanted to defend herself, and yet she knew that what Rob was saying made so much sense. Her spending was out of control, and her marriage was in jeopardy. She'd been preparing for this day for a long time and, in a way, she was relieved to be finally facing things head on.

"Why don't I start?" she said. "I can see that this is just the same old pattern I've had all my life. It seems like when I see some clothes I want, I have no ability to wait for them until we can afford them. I think it's a way of escaping my problems and my feelings. I mean, shopping is almost like a drug for me. It gives me a high—and it'll definitely be hard to give up!"

Jane sees the store.
The store is big.
See Jane look. See Jane walk.
Jane is walking home!

Think and Discuss

1. When have you resisted making a change that someone wanted? What were your reasons?

2. In what areas of your life have you long wanted to change but weren't sure where to start?

3. What is your reaction to the story of the potholes in the road? How do you typically deal with a pothole in your own life? Why?

4. What would your spouse say about your "maturity in love"? If you were to "grow up" a bit more in the coming months, how, specifically, would you be different? How might these changes affect your marital relationship?

Implementing Your "Marriage Makeover" Plan

Note: Each spouse should take time, in advance, to jot his or her responses to the questions on a separate sheet of paper before coming together for sharing and discussion.

"Growing Up" Step #1:
Moving from Discouragement to Possibility.

Key task: *While learning from the past, make a solid, mutual commitment to change in the future.*

1. Review the chapter-opening stories of Dick and Jane.

• *Husband, be Jane for a moment. Describe some of the feelings weighing upon your heart:*

• *Wife, be Dick. Tell what you are feeling, and why:*

• *Discuss your perceptions together. To what extent do you agree and disagree about what's happening within the two spouses and their marriages?*

2. Take some time to tell one another about yourselves, related to key chapter themes. Complete these sentences:

• *The most bothersome "patterned behaviors" I've noticed in my life so far have been . . .*

• *The typical way I attempt to escape my pain is . . .*

• *For me to begin "owning my stuff," I'd need to focus on . . .*

3. I would describe my current level of "marital discouragement" as:

1_____2_____3_____4_____5

Totally Depressed   Upbeat

4. When it comes to the possibility of change in our marriage, my attitude is:

1_____2_____3_____4_____5
No way, Baby!   Bring it on, Kid!

5. In a perfect world . . .

* *Here is my ideal vision for the future with my spouse:*

* *Here are some reasons I think this vision could become reality:*

6. Do some brainstorming together. List some of the possible obstacles to change in your marriage:

His List   **Her List**

7. Now look over your list and discuss:

* *A first step we could take toward overcoming one of these obstacles would be to . . .*

8. Jot down the specific commitment you're making. Talk about forms of accountability you could use. What would help you keep this commitment?

2 Being So Self-Centered!

S ee Jane go.
See Jane do her own thing.
See Dick go too.
Come back, Jane! Come back, Dick!

At the end of the previous chapter, we imagined the first steps toward a happier marriage for our two couples, Dick and Linda, Rob and Jane. But we were observing merely with our mind's eye . . . with incredibly high hopes!

In reality, Dick and Linda continue to struggle. Yes, they try to talk about their problems, but they usually end up blaming each other. Tempers flare. Linda, totally exasperated, says she will soon give up on talking to Dick.

Jane and Rob are doing no better. While their story is a little different, they too are suffering fallout from being stuck in patterned behaviors of the past. Jane, as you may recall, was having a tough time seeing the need to give up her spending habits. She rationalized they were both too young to worry about saving. On one occasion, when they were fighting about the issue once again, she even accused Rob of "being too old for your age." Ouch!

Dick and Jane, like you and me, have grown up physically. From all outward appearances they have matured and are ready to face life's great chal-

Technical Talk

Narcissus Still Lives!

In psychological circles, it's well known that self-preoccupation leads to dysfunctional living. This is the problem of *narcissism*. Here's a fuller explanation:

Narcissism, or self-absorption, takes many forms. Some are normal in childhood but not in adulthood. Some are more distinctly pathological than others. Malignant narcissism is characterized by an unsubmitted will.

But adults who are mentally healthy submit themselves, one way or another, to something higher than themselves, be it God, or truth, or love, or some other ideal. They do what God wants them to do rather than what they desire.[1]

lenges. But are they? Have they indeed matured intellectually, emotionally, spiritually?

One way to find out is to check the "Me Factor" in their lives. In other words, one of the hallmarks of adult maturity is the ability to move from a purely self-focused life toward a focus on the welfare of the beloved. It's the blessed, happy movement from "me" to "we."

Are You Living a "ME"-Focused Life?

Most of us are products of what has been called "The Me Generation." We've heard, time and again, "If it feels good, do it." Or, "Look out for number one." Or, "Let others fend for themselves." We've been raised to believe that we are the center of the universe. Our pain and pleasure are the most important things in life. Yet how our vision narrows when we focus so intensely on what makes us feel good while de-emphasizing caring for others!

Experiencing the commercially driven cultural values of our time, it is no wonder that Dick and Jane face problems in their respective marriages. Selfish pursuits in the name of "individualism" do create marital pitfalls. And since this is such a great danger, let's be sure we know the warning signs of a me-focused life. What, exactly does it look like? Consider the following three characteristics of "ME living":

Striving for the Pinnacle of Success

" don't have a problem," she said. "I just want to make enough to buy that new BMW that came out last year. If I had that, I'd be able to work more effectively with my well-to-do clientele. It's not really to feed my ego, you understand. It's a tax-deductible part of the job."

Actually, we've all been attracted in one way or another to the finer things of life. I've lusted after a Waterman fountain pen and a leather travel kit myself. But, we must be brave. This newest allurement could be just another diversion to draw our attention away from our relationship to our spouse—or God. In We must learn to set limits on our desires, so we can discover what truly satisfies. As William Blake once quipped: "You never know what is enough unless you know what is more than enough."

You may be thinking: "I've worked hard to keep my life in balance. I've gone to workshops on how to combine my work life with my family life. I know it's tricky, but I'm the one who can do it. So, what's wrong with that?" Well, perhaps you are the one who can do it. For most, if not all, this seeking of wealth and advancement becomes all-consuming, attached to a price tag that comes due at the most unexpected times. But when the dream of "having it all" is held before us, no one talks about the price. Who tells us it will take so much time and energy that we will only have bits and pieces of ourselves left to give back to those we love?

> # Danger Here!
>
> You can know you have a narrow vision and are caught up in purely selfish pursuits if:
>
> You spend the bulk of your energies dreaming about potential accomplishments rather than planning for what's best for your primary relationships;
>
> You constantly manipulate situations to get what you want;
>
> You have difficulty owning up to your limitations when you're wrong;
>
> You find that asking forgiveness is next to impossible;
>
> You "forget" to compliment those near to you, ignoring their accomplishments and failing to express your admiration and appreciation;
>
> You hardly notice when your significant others need something from you;
>
> You begin taking your most important relationships for granted.

In my own life, coming out of graduate school, I had no one telling me how to build a practice while raising a family. Too often I erred in the direction of throwing all my energies into my work at the expense of my home life. My focus became far too narrow—which I can only fully see through the rearview mirror. I look back now and see the years I missed in our children's early, formative years. I have regrets. It makes me think of a statement from former First Lady Barbara Bush: "At the end of your life, you will never regret not having passed one more test, not winning one more verdict or not closing one more deal. You will regret time not spent with a husband, a friend, a child or a parent. . . . No one ever came to the end of life saying 'I wish I'd spent more time at the office.'"

Nevertheless, we're bombarded daily with media images of success that take place only at the office. We are told repeatedly that we can have it all, if we are willing to work for it. In fact, the lie is quite believable. Yet, inside, most of us know that something immeasurably precious will be lost if we pursue the dream with the fierce determination that's required.

Obsessing about Youth and Beauty

Now let me see all the hands of those who want to talk about aging and its impact on our appearance and self-esteem. Can I see those hands? Higher, please.

Okay, so it's a little hard to talk about.

Another desperate, selfish search for meaning and happiness takes the form of our adoration of youth and the perfect body. Many of us have become so preoccupied with this admiration of physical health that, again, *the Self becomes the center of existence*.

A woman named Trish came to me, concerned about her anorexic eating disorder. She was well aware of the self-destruction she was causing, yet she felt powerless to change. Having grown up in a family where she received constant criticism, she still carried emotional pain that she tried to salve by maintaining a perfectly honed physique. As she grew older it became increasingly difficult to keep the cellulite off, and soon she began taking drastic measures such as using laxatives and vomiting to keep her weight down. By the time she saw me she was very discouraged.

Trish had kept her problem a secret from everyone, though her husband had his suspicions and had asked her for some time to get help. However, embarrassed by her actions, she wanted to keep the silence. This, unfortunately, gave the addiction-to-thinness even more power over her. Her courageous step forward in talking with me was her start in overcoming the problem. She is now learning to face her inner pain, working on old family messages, teaming up with a group of women working on their own eating disorders. Her prognosis is good.

Frequently the adoration-of-youth person comes in the form of a "Peter Pan." Utterly delightful for a while, this charming playmate can become a pain in marriage. These Peters and Pams want to play continuously. They refuse to grow up or take responsibility. Relationships should, they rationalize, fit into their plans, their schedules. "You only go around once," they say. There is always some new toy to occupy this oversized child who prefers ongoing distraction to the toils of routine daily family life. However, for the spouse left waiting at the empty dinner table or wondering where hubby or wife is tonight, this oversized child's form of self-worship becomes tiresome, indeed.

Escaping into Addictions

Even before reading about the adventures of Dick and Jane, most of us were taught, innocently enough, that if we had an ache or pain anywhere, our moms and dads could fix it. They showed us that we could stick something into our mouths to make just about any kind of pain go away. And it worked nearly every time. In addition to medicines, we learned of a plethora of remedies to "make us feel better."

Now we have an entire generation that finds it easy to escape discomfort by ingesting some substance or other. Observing that we have a tough time simply living with the normal pains of life, M. Scott Peck notes that the problem is twofold: First, we can never avoid pain, since it is part of our existence; second, when we repeatedly attempt to avoid pain, our pattern of behavior becomes compulsive and, thereby, destructive.

One of the hallmarks of addictive and compulsive behavior is that it becomes terribly self-centered. Our lives begin to revolve around finding

Danger Here!
Defining Addiction

Put simply, an addiction is any mood-altering substance, experience, or person that . . .

- you rely on for nurturing;
- you trust;
- gives you an artificial sense of self-sufficiency;
- allows you to organize your life;
- keeps you from knowing and feeling a deeper, unresolved hunger;
- gives you the illusion of perfect control.

Considering these warning signs, are you one of the addicted? Any addiction to alcohol or drugs? approval? rage? work? love? shame? church? chocolate? television? food? sex? money? excitement? illness? shopping?

Would you like to stop but can't? Would you like to change, but you stay the same?

ways to take away the pain. Consider the workaholic, how he or she uses all kinds of excuses to continue a single-minded drive toward success, fame, or some other illusive goal. Remember that *the ultimate goal is a change of mood.* It's as if the tail wags the dog. The drive replaces the goal. The workaholic climber on the wobbly ladder to success loses his or her focus in a side-search for the next "high."

Or perhaps you know substance abusers who use alcohol or drugs excessively. Looking for creative ways to hide their insecurities, these abusers are in search of self-esteem or a painless way to change their mood. The "typical" addict is less likely to be the stereotypical drunk; more likely he or she sits in a Dilbert-lined cubicle at a respectable office or drives a pickup to a well-paying job site. Those around them—who love and try to support them— are left out of their decisions. Pleading and caretaking do nothing to alter the process. In fact, the pleading only serves to focus more energy on the addict, until all of the family's energies and resources are exhausted.

Drugs, alcohol, sex, work, shopping, politicking, eating, not eating, gambling—the list of potential excesses goes on and on. For them, *the feeding of the enthroned Self is the focus of life.* All other needs, commitments, relationships must take a backseat until there is a "breakdown" leading to change. But, change they must if their marriages are to survive.

Those who live with a significantly addicted person know that a relationship cannot grow while the addiction is alive and well. In time the addict's partner recognizes that his or her marital energies can only funnel into an ever-narrowing vision unless the addicted partner's heart changes. With a new vision, partners may emerge from their emotional and spiritual quagmire.

If you believe you might have an addiction problem, I urge you to seek outside assistance to determine the extent of your problem. Please do not deceive yourself with unfounded optimism. After over twenty years' experience, I know that it will do no good to evaluate your life alone, without input from trusted others. Caught in the web of denial, you will be unable to see your issues clearly.

We find aspects of the three "ME factors" unfolding in the lives of our prototype couples. Hopefully, though, Dick and Linda as well as Jane and Rob will seek help—perhaps through marriage counseling or through seminars and small groups offered at their churches. Thus they'll be able to identify issues, analyze their motivations, face their pain and longings directly, and arrive at a new, "we centered" vision.

Isn't that your vision too?

Would You Like a "WE"-Centered Marriage?

A short time ago a woman and her husband were in my office for a much-needed couples' counseling session. The husband didn't want to be there. His crossed arms and glower clearly indicated his disgust at the "wasted" time and expense, not to mention his personal embarrassment at being in a "shrink's" office.

Recognizing his discomfort, I told an amusing story.

No response.

So I asked if he were comfortable.

No response.

Could I get them a cup of coffee?

No response.

So I shared the story of how uncomfortable I'd been when my wife insisted I attend one of her medical examinations. Talk about embarrassment!

Ever so slowly, the man began to recognize his wife's need and to thaw to the idea of listening to someone for advice. Thus we inched along into the therapy hour. At one poignant moment in their session, the woman paused and haltingly shared her frustration with how little she received from her husband emotionally. Tearfully she said, "What do you think would happen if you focused as much on our marriage, and me, as you do on your work?"

Wow! You could have heard a pin drop, and I was stopped in my tracks as well. It was one of those illuminating "light bulb" moments.

Of course this question threw the man off. He wanted to become defensive but kept hearing a little voice inside telling him to keep listening. Still, I could see he was debating whether to bolt for the door or hear what else his wife had to say. Although it didn't feel like a safe place for him, he had the courage to stay.

He stayed and he listened.

He took the first step toward saving his marriage.

There is a time when we must—if we are going to have a satisfying marriage—move from "me" to "we." When that happens, certain new characteristics begin showing up in the relationship, as we and our spouses learn and grow. We begin noticing that we are, more and more, in a marriage that is . . .

. . . Guided by a Giving Spirit

In a renewing marriage, a spirit of giving (instead of taking) begins to flow. It is a spirit of generosity that flows from the heart, of giving until it hurts, of giving with no expectation of return.

We will dwell on this topic extensively in a coming chapter, but for now, I can't think of a better illustration of self-sacrificial giving than the story of the young boy who was asked whether he'd give a pint of blood for his sister after her surgery. While frightened, he courageously consented. He was unsure of what to expect, but at the hospital the nurse ushered him into a room and asked him to lie down. She tried to calm his trembling and then began drawing the blood. After a few quiet moments, the little boy, through a stiff upper lip, asked: "How soon will I die?"

Can we lay down our lives—our precious egos—for our spouses?

The Apostle Paul demonstrated this kind of selflessness in that his entire life's mission involved giving his life away. He didn't squander it selfishly but knew that if he pursued God's goals for him he would bring others into God's kingdom and—as a fantastic side benefit—find true happiness himself. His life illustrated that the secret of contentment and peace is to focus on Christ—the

Danger Here!
Giving Comfort

A little girl was sent on an early errand by her mother, but she took far too much time to return home. When she finally did return, her mother wanted to know what had taken so long. The little girl explained that on the way she had met a little friend who was crying because she had broken her doll. "Oh," said the mother, "then you stopped to help her fix the doll?" "Oh, no," replied the little girl, "I stopped to help her cry."

This little girl knew exactly what her friend needed. When people are hurting, they need comfort. But here is the danger: We often respond to a hurting [spouse] in unproductive ways—

We offer logic: "The reason that happened was..."
We offer advice: "Next time, do it this way..."
We give a pep-talk: "You're a winner, you'll survive!"
We try to fix things: "I know what to do, let me..."

When all the while, what our spouse truly wants and needs is simple, old-fashioned comfort.[2]

supreme example of servanthood. In fact, Paul pursued the same passion that motivated Christ in His ultimate self-sacrifice. His approach to life was this:

Do nothing from selfish ambition or conceit, but in humility regard others as better than yourselves. Let each of you look not to your own interests, but to the interests of others. Let the same mind be in you that was in Christ Jesus, who, though he was in the form of God, did not regard equality with God as something to be exploited, but emptied himself, taking the form of a slave, being born in human likeness. And being found in human form, he humbled himself and became obedient to the point of death—even death on a cross.
—Philippians 2:3-8

Suppose each spouse were to follow the path of humble servanthood in the marriage relationship? The point is this: As we determine to follow God's values and break out of our own limited vision, we can then live according to His mission, which includes serving others. I believe that putting our spouse's needs ahead of our own will revolutionize our marital relationships. Time and again, I've observed it to be true.

. . . Committed to *True* Self-Care

Unfortunately, so many of the me-centered activities (discussed in the first half of this chapter) disguise themselves in the costume of "self-caring." They are anything but that! Such compulsive activities, *externally oriented*, lead to the lack of true self-care. Real self-care requires a balance of work and play; of rest and activity; of reflection with movement. We all know that self-care requires a balance of outer pursuits with inner pursuits. We need to be alone at times, and totally committed to intimacy at other times. When we fail to honor this delicate balance something will eventually break down.

Our efforts to find peace through purely external, childish pursuits, totally miss the mark. We can reach our goal of maturity only through an internal, spiritual process. Attempting to find completeness through any other source, such as personal prestige, the approval of others, or a great appearance will lead to disappointment and frustration. Even if we make it to the top of the success ladder, we'll likely find that it was resting against the wrong wall. As C.S. Lewis once commented: "What does not satisfy when we find it, was not the thing we were desiring."

We do desire something higher, something transcendent—a spiritual connection with God and with our spouses too. Sadly, what often appears as self-care is actually self-absorption in disguise.

Self-Check
How Well Am I Taking Care of Myself?

Healthy self-care means nurturing yourself with things that "fill your tank," physically, emotionally, and spiritually. A wonderful benefit of taking care of yourself this way is that you build up reserves from which you can draw as you give of yourself to your spouse. It's hard to give from an empty tank!

So, for your own good, and the good of your spouse, begin asking yourself the questions below.

• How much rest and sleep am I allowing myself each day?

• What forms of exercise do I engage in regularly?

• How would I describe my eating habits? Am I getting the best nutrition, or do I frequently binge on fast foods?

• How much "personal space"—alone time and free time—do I have in my days?

• What friendships am I enjoying these days?

• What "creative outlets" do I have in my life right now—things I do that make my life interesting, and that tap into my special abilities?

• How have I been cultivating my relationship with God—doing things that nurture my soul?

• What other things do I need in my life in order to be whole, healthy, and growing?

As you ponder your responses, why not jot them on a separate sheet of paper—or in your personal journal—and share them with your mate?[3]

. . . Motivated by Mature Expectations

As we watch Dick and Linda lose ground in their marriage, it is clear that an early childhood pattern—the "me first" attitude—is at the root of the havoc. Each counts on the other spouse to meet his or her expectations. Several devastating symptoms of marital disease can flow from such unrealistic expectations, but let me just highlight one of them here: a growing, festering resentment in the marriage.

Resentment has been defined as "the difference between expectations and reality." In other words, when we expect one thing and have strong beliefs about it, if we receive something apparently less, we will probably feel resentment. This resentment, *when not dealt with directly*, will not simply dissipate and go away. Allowed to linger, it can create physical and emotional problems such as tension headaches, stomach upsets, and a malaise much like a depression. It can also produce relational problems such as sexual detachment.

Resentment reveals selfish demands. For example, Dick and Linda each selfishly expected the other to make their differences go away. When we get to the point of feeling resentment, which is important to acknowledge, we are usually rehearsing how wronged we have been and how unfairly the other person has acted toward us. We tend to see things in black and white, right and wrong (more about blaming in another chapter). Resentment is the feeling that says *we should not have to feel this way*, and it is up to our spouse to change so that we no longer have these feelings.

But the fact is: *we alone are responsible for our feelings*.

If there is a positive side to all of this, it's the fact that resentment can also be a signal to us, like anger, that something is wrong. It certainly indicates a relational issue needing attention. Actually, that is the blessing-in-disguise of virtually any pain—it is a call to change our ways.

But that is a good thing! We've seen that living a me-focused life can give way to a we-focused marriage. It takes courage and persistence to move from me to we, and it may call for some drastic changes in attitude and lifestyle. But the reward, in terms of deepened intimacy—and the restoration of a good portion of the original "fun" and romance in the relationship—is well worth the effort.

Will Dick and Jane be able to grow in these ways?

Let's imagine it.

See Dick and Jane Grow Up

Life can be a series of distractions until something occurs that brings us clarity. Both Dick and Jane found themselves wondering about how their marriage was going and the risks they both faced if they did not change. They knew their changes must begin on the inside. Both truly desired changes in their attitudes and vision, not just in their circumstances.

Imagine a Heart-Change in Dick . . .

Dick had been musing for days about Linda's recent moods and how he might approach her one more time. Because he was afraid of how she might react, he'd been avoiding her. He could sense her slipping away, their marriage along with her. He didn't want to ignore the problem any longer.

"Linda," Dick said hesitantly. "I want to talk about what's happening between us. Can we talk?"

"Okay," she said receptively.

"Well, I know that I've been a jerk lately. I don't really want to change and yet I know that is what I have to do. To be honest, much of me still resists doing what I know is right. But I don't want to lose you, and our marriage is more important than my buddies. I'm not so sure how good they are for me anyway."

"Dick, you know I've begun creating my own life away from you. I don't think I've helped things a whole lot. I felt that I couldn't count on you anymore and decided to do my own thing. That hasn't been the best for us. So I'm partly to blame too."

"Yeah," he said. "I could sense you pulling away. I can't say that I've liked it, but I can't blame you. If I make myself more available to you, will you spend more of your time with me?"

"Sure," Linda said, smiling. "What would you think about us going in for a little counseling?"

"Ooh," Dick said, wincing. "Are things that bad? I was hoping you wouldn't ask me to do that. I can't say I'd be excited about it, but I'd be willing to go if you think it might be the best thing."

Linda paused before speaking. "I know that I'm asking a lot, but I'd like you to commit to going for a few sessions. I don't want to go and have you feel uncomfortable and beg out. Would you commit to going?"

"Yes, I will," Dick said firmly. "You are certainly worth that to me."

Imagine a Heart-Change in Jane . . .

Jane had been thinking about her "childhood issues." A recent visit to her parents' home had brought some painful experiences to the surface again. She caught her father "preaching" at her. However, instead of lashing out at him as in the past, she took him aside and quietly talked about her feelings. She was surprised at how well he listened and even more surprised when he agreed to attempt changing the way he related to her.

Jane had always assumed that her relationship with her father would keep making her feel like a child—and that she'd continue to resent it. Through the counsel of her pastor she had worked on preparing to talk with him "in an adult way." That is, she would invite him to communicate with her in the same manner. While she was doubtful, she felt it was worth a try.

"I can't believe the discussion I had with my dad tonight," Jane told Rob as they drove home. "It felt like we had a real breakthrough. He listened to me instead of preaching at me. He told me how much he loved me and said he'd always treated me like a child because of his need to protect me. But he apologized and said he would work on it."

"That's great, Jane," Rob said, touching her hand while keeping the other gripped on the wheel. "I really like your dad and know he cares a lot for you. I don't know about his past, but I think it's hard for him not to be critical. Sounds like you had a breakthrough for sure."

"I'm hoping that it will help you and me too," Jane continued with tears in her eyes. "I don't want to fight against you. I think I've been resisting any kind of discipline in my life. Maybe in some ways I clung to being treated like a child at home; I guess it was less scary because it demanded a whole lot less confrontation with my parents. I mean, it was just easier to go along with them.

"But I don't want to be a little kid in this marriage. You're my husband, not my dad! And I want to be more sensitive to our relationship. Will you help me with it?"

Rob smiled and took her hand. "This isn't a one-way street, Honey. I need to change some things too. How about if we work on things together?"

Think and Discuss

1. How much of your daily energy is devoted to deepening your marriage relationship as compared to pursuing other goals?

2. Do you have any addictions that have stunted your emotional and spiritual growth? What would likely happen if you tried to discuss this with your spouse?

3. From your point of view, what has been the main distraction from intimacy in your marriage?

4. What practical steps are you, personally, willing to take to move from "me" to "we"?

5. List and discuss the *benefits* of making such a move. What might be the *costs?*

Strategy Step
Prepare a Manual on Your Spouse

Since his (or her) mother is unlikely to provide you with a suitable booklet describing all his special likes and needs, you will have to construct your own! You will suffer fewer breakdowns and experience higher performance if you understand how his or her machine works!

How to do it? Consciously study your partner and learn what makes him or her tick. Ask certain key questions about your partner:

• When are her down hours during the day?
• What kind of food does he particularly like?
• What subjects is she sensitive about?
• What weekend activity will put him in high gear?
• How can I feed my partner's self-esteem?
• How does he really feel about criticism?
• What frightens her?

The list goes on. . . . Maybe you'd like to add some questions that are important to you.[4]

Implementing Your "Marriage Makeover" Plan

Note: Each spouse should take time, in advance, to jot his or her responses to these questions on a separate sheet of paper before coming together for sharing and discussion.

"Growing Up" Step #2:
Moving from Me to We

Key task: *Determine to treat your spouse as a beloved partner rather than a live-in competitor.*

1. Discuss the role of the "Me" Factor in your marriage. (Be sure to check your perceptions with your spouse!)

• *The Top 3 areas in my life where the "Me" Factor seems most obvious these days:*

_____   _____   _____

• *One area in which I see the "Me Factor" operating in my spouse these days:*

_____

2. Complete the following sentences:

• *My main EXPECTATION in our relationship is . . .*

- *My spouse would likely say this expectation is (circle one):*
reasonable / unreasonable.

- *The probable reason why my spouse would say this is:*

• *My main RESENTMENT in our relationship is . . .*

- *My spouse would likely say this resentment is (circle one):*
reasonable / unreasonable.

- The probable reason why my spouse would say this is:

3. For a few minutes, think about your needs and the needs of your spouse in this marriage. Share your responses to the questions below, letting the discussion move in directions that will be most helpful to you. (Note: Make it your goal to listen intently while avoiding any defensiveness.)

- *What are my main needs?*

- *Which of my needs do I feel are being overlooked or ignored in the marriage?*

- *What would my spouse say are his or her main needs?*

- *Which of these needs would my spouse say are being overlooked or ignored?*

4. In what specific way would I like my mate to try meeting one of my stated needs?

5. What practical steps could I take to begin meeting one of my spouse's stated needs in a fuller way?

6. One way I could begin treating my spouse more as a partner than a competitor would be for me to . . .

7. Agree on a plan together in which you promise to take turns "giving" to one another during the next month (with no expectation of return). How would this work for you?

3 Launching Another Attack

See Dick and Jane fight.
Are Dick and Jane happy?
No, Dick is not happy.
Look! Jane is not happy.

"Must be nice to lie around," she said.

It had been a quiet Sunday afternoon at Dick and Linda's house. Both had enjoyed the church service and Linda was preparing a casserole for lunch. Their two young children had already been fed and were down for an afternoon nap. Dick took the opportunity to catch up on the Sunday paper. He'd just taken his shoes off and put his feet on the ottoman when Linda walked by him briskly.

She headed for the kitchen to continue cutting up the chicken for their casserole. Dick imagined her from his chair as he listened to the cleaver methodically thumping against the cutting block.

"Say, Linda," Dick called out. "I think the chicken is dead. No need to butcher it again."

With that, Linda rushed into the living room waving a chicken leg she had been cutting.

"Dick, why am I out there cooking and you're in here reading? Is there anything wrong with this picture? I'm beat. I was up late studying, went to church, got the kids their lunch, and put them down for a nap. Now I'm supposed to baby you?"

"Whoa!" Dick shouted. "Just a minute. You missed a few steps. You left out the part about me helping bathe the kids this morning. You forgot to add that I prepared for teaching Sunday School last night and this morning. You overlooked how I ran into the store on the way home to get the food for lunch. Is this feel-sorry-for-Linda time? And one last thing: You could have asked me to help, you know, if it was that big of a deal."

"It's the attitude that causes me problems. You're the reason I'm so tired. You think you help but you don't. I'm sick of it."

* * * *

"What do you think about going to the beach this Saturday?" Rob asked Jane as they sat on their deck enjoying the summer evening. "It's supposed to be a great tide for clams."

Jane hesitated. She had told him the night before that she wanted to go to Portland for the weekend with her friends. But he'd obviously forgotten.

"Do you remember our conversation last night?" she asked. "Do you recall what I said I was doing this Friday night?"

Rob looked puzzled. He stroked his temples instinctively as if to jog his memory. "You didn't tell me anything about other plans. I would have remembered if you had."

"Actually," Jane continued, "do you remember that I was planning on going to Portland for the night with Betsy and Lila? Does that ring any bells?"

"No, it doesn't," Rob said. "If you had told me you were going to Portland on some ladies-only shopping spree, I'd have told you what I thought about it! I don't want you going anywhere with those two squanderers. Why in the world do you want to be influenced by them? That's all we need in our home."

"Just a minute," Jane said. "You're not being fair. They haven't done anything to you. Why are you attacking them? Nice way of getting the focus off of you, since we talked about all of this last night."

Rob turned and headed back into the house.

"Let me know when I can fit into your life again."

Living in a War Zone

Every day, in millions of homes, marriages are destroyed, angry word by angry word. It's as if the couple has decided to enter into war with one another; thus, they establish firmly defended battlelines, employ the occasional sneak attack, resort to all-out bombing raids, or pull back for a period of "cold war" (with the threat of brutal guerilla action at any moment). A gradual loss of intimacy is the result.

How does it happen? What factors produce this kind of adversarial environment at home? I believe it has to do with something important about (1) our *needs* and (2) our *thoughts*.

Needing to Attack

Sitting in my office in consultation with a couple on a late Thursday afternoon, I felt a tight queasiness in my chest. From the beginning, the couple had agreed on nothing. They sniped at one another like professional marksmen. They were so good that for a little while I'd been lulled into just watching their skillful, passive-aggressive combat maneuvers.

Actually, I could see that it was really a "game"—attack/counter-attack. No matter the topic, they took turns torpedoing each other's ideas. With disdainful scoffing, they conveyed the underlying message that their partner was always at fault. Things would be fine if the other would simply see things the "right" way.

I intervened at this point. "Can I talk to both of you for a few moments? Is what I'm seeing right now typical of what happens in your home behind closed doors?"

Both rang out in unison, "Yes!"

He added, "This garbage happens all the time. We can't talk for more than two minutes before we're at each other's throats."

"Well, I have good news and bad news to share with you," I said with a big grin. There was a certain humor in this desperate situation. "What would you like first?" I asked.

"Give us the good news," she said. "We could use some good news about now."

"Well," I said, feeling I had at last left the war zone. "The good news is that you two actually do agree on something very important to your relationship: *You do seem to think that attacking and blaming each other will have a positive effect on your marriage.*"

They looked at one another soberly, while he added, "No, we don't think

Danger Here!

The Purpose of Blame

If you are caught on the treadmill of blame, you're serving some inner purpose. But we can walk off a treadmill any time we choose; it's not a cage. We are not shackled hand or foot. Look at the following list and see if one or more of these keeps you from setting yourself free:

Blaming others helps us avoid making decisions.

Blaming others helps us feel sorry for ourselves.

Blaming others helps us distance ourselves from our mates.

Blaming others helps us hold off being kind.

Blaming others helps us manipulate others.

Blaming others helps us take the spotlight off our mistakes.

Blaming others helps us hide behind our own insecurities.

Blaming others helps us hold back mercy, grace, and forgiveness.[1]

our fighting is doing any good. We know it's tearing us apart. But it's almost as if we need to do it. Like it's a habit with us. By the way, if that was the good news, I hate to hear the bad news."

"You already said it. The fighting is tearing you two apart. You still have a lot of good left in your marriage, but it's buried beneath all of this hurt and anger that comes as a result of attacking and blaming one another. If we can work on that, you two will have a head start on rebuilding your marriage."

Of course, few of us consciously set out to undermine our partners. Perhaps you remember your courting days, those blissful evenings together that you thought would never end. But end they did. Although we go to great lengths to forestall returning to the harsher realities of everyday life, our routine responsibilities intrude— sometimes with a loud thud.

When this happens, we're surprised that her cute giggle wears on us and starts to seem "childish." That his pouting, which earlier was a reason for teasing, is now silly and "intolerable." As bills go unpaid for lack of enough money, each sees his or her mate's "extravagant" habits as the reason for slapping controls on the other"s spending. What a difference a few months make! It could even lead to a few significant battles.

But does reality have to damage all of the good feeling and optimism that so buoyed a couple such a short time ago? The answer is "yes" and "no." Yes, reality usually has to hit that hard. It is no fun, but the balloon of magical love was overinflated.

The other answer is "no." Reality does not have to erode all of the good feelings that you had for one another. But to hang onto the good feelings, several things are required. You must learn not to do those things that subtly attack the good. And you must keep adding to the emotional bank account of affection. No rocket science here!

But why, exactly, do we so often feel compelled to attack our spouses in the first place? Let me suggest three basic reasons:

First, we feel a need to attack because that's what we learned to do in our family of origin. Long before our own family came into being, Adam and Eve did a pretty good job of passing the buck. That doesn't let us off the hook, but it does help us to understand what's happening. Many of us have grown up in families that didn't model good communication skills. We may have watched our parents yell and scream at one another when they were upset. Perhaps they didn't follow any "fair fighting" principles; it was a "free-for-all." The one with the loudest voice won. In this world of family chaos, we were too young to see how dysfunctional it all was. So our need to attack may simply spring from the learning we absorbed from years of parental "instruction" by example. Only now are we able to look back and see the craziness for what it was.

Second, we feel a need to attack when we're at a loss for words. Growing up, many of us never learned how to talk about what is hurting us and why. It's important to talk because sometimes a hurt derives from a misunderstanding. Or maybe it is misplaced anger, bubbling up from an issue that is totally un-related to our marital relationship. But if our angry words simply burst forth to relieve that kind of inner pressure, our mate won't have a clue. So ask yourself some questions: Why am I hurting? What set this pain in motion? Be honest. Find an effective way to share with your mate about this pain, without slinging mud.

Third, we feel a need to attack when we're forced to face painful truths. In other words, we may be acting on the old sports proverb that "a good offense is the best defense." When we feel vulnerable, fearing we'll have to let down and bare our souls, we choose to launch an attack instead.

Most of us do live with a façade that covers our true selves to some degree. We have an outward persona that we exhibit to the world and an inner self known only to ourselves. (Sometimes that inner self isn't very well known to us, either). It can be very disconcerting when someone, like our mate, suddenly sees through our façade and challenges us. *We become vulnerable because we have been exposed.* If we don't feel good about ourselves, we won't want to be exposed.

Danger Here!

Unfair Fighting—*Ouch!*

When you face conflict with your spouse, do you fight fair? In the exercise below, you'll explore seven of the most common unfair fighting tactics.

- **Universalizing:** Making an unwarranted leap from a specific situation to a vast generalization. (Often makes use of "always" and "never.")

Example: "You're holding the garage sale *tomorrow?* Women are all alike—they never take the time to plan things out in a logical, organized way."

- Character Killing: Switching from the issues of the conflict to making a personal attack on your spouse. (May include sarcasm for more devastating effect.)

Example: "Oh, yeah? I think it's pretty obvious you're not exactly a Wall Street genius when it comes to handling the family's finances!"

- **Cloud-covering:** Making a vague, foggy accusation instead of being detailed and specific about a complaint. (Again, sarcasm helps!)

Example: "Hmmm ... so I'm going to have the pleasure of enjoying your driving again? That should be ... *interesting.*"

- **Uping the Ante:** Instead of responding to the hurt or anger of your spouse, you just play "tit-for-tat" by citing a worse case that's been done to you.

Example: "You think forgetting your birthday is bad? What about when you forgot my graduation?"

- **Scatter-bombing:** Dropping into the conversation a huge list of sins (usually unrelated)—including everything *and* the kitchen sink!

Example: "Yes, I may have been wrong. But you've been late before, and you bought all those tools without asking me, and remember you forgot to bring milk home yesterday, and you insulted my mother just last week, plus you quit your job that time, and furthermore ... etc., etc. ..."

- **Moth-balling:** Putting an old grievance in storage—for years or decades—and bringing it out at just the right time to hurt your spouse.

Example: "You think I hurt *you?* Well Sally, I hate to bring it up, but remember the time back in 1986 when you had that little so-called 'business function' with Harry?"

- **Spitting-in-your-soup:** Using passive-aggressive comments to lay the guilt on the other party. Often involves sarcasm.

Example: "No problem; you guys go ahead and play your 64 holes of golf. Have a great time! I'll just stay home and take care of your Mom."[2]

In Linda's case, she was avoiding exposure of a childhood incidence of sexual abuse, something that had caused her much pain, even into adulthood. Similarly, all of us have hidden frailties, perhaps even those that we were taunted about as children, come flying back at us in a hostile way. If harsh words are spoken at a time when our defenses are down, it hurts! It's like having a bandage ripped off, leaving our wound exposed.

The bottom line is that it's incredibly hard to listen to critical feedback without becoming defensive. We have little tolerance for an opinion different from our own, especially if our own position is shored up by a strong commitment—politically, religiously, financially—or touches on an old "sore point." Such challenges feel like a sword point pressing too near the heart.

Thinking in Black-and-White Extremes

Not only do our *needs* get in the way of peace in a marriage; our faulty ways of *thinking* contribute to an "attack environment," as well. You see, when we were children the world was quite simple for us. We saw things in black and white instead of Technicolor. Studies of mental functioning tell us that at early ages we aren't yet capable of abstract reasoning. If something disappears from sight, it no longer exists. If something appears to be taller, while in fact it is shorter, in the child's mind it is still taller. At that age we have very little ability to understand different perspectives.

Therefore, black-and-white thinking says that my way is the right way. So, if we get into a disagreement, you must be wrong. If you are wrong, I am going to be righteously indignant and try to dissuade you from your position. This will be a win/lose proposition with the ultimate goal being, of course, that I win. Unfortunately, there can only be one winner, and it's no fun to lose.

Robert Fulgham, in *All I Really Need to Know I Learned in Kindergarten*, tells of sitting by the fireside with a group of kids playing a boisterous game of Old Maid. "A flock of moths were cork-screwing around the Coleman lantern. Every once in a while one would hit the hot spot and go zzssshh and spin out and crash like a fighter plane in a bad combat movie."

He notes that the kids enjoyed this scene and began, themselves, to roll up sheets of newspaper, killing more moths.

"I leapt to the defense of the moths. It's bad enough that the lantern hypnotizes them into kamikaze runs and that spiders zap them into lunch meat, but small boys with newspapers are excessive handicaps to have to overcome."

"Why are you killing the poor moths?"

"Moths are *bad*," says he.

"Everybody knows *that*," shouts another.

"Sure, moths eat your clothes."

"I could not sway them. *All* moths are *bad*. All butterflies are *good*. Period. Moths and butterflies are not the same thing. Moths sneak around in the dark munching your sweater and are ugly. Butterflies hang out with flowers in the daytime and are pretty. Never mind any facts or what silkworm moths are responsible for, or what poisonous butterflies do. With a firmness that would have made John Calvin proud, moths were condemned, now and forevermore, amen. Out of the mouths of babes may come gems of wisdom, but also garbage."[3]

It's the problem of black-and-white, extreme thinking! I sometimes think of it as a person acting like a "dog with a bone." The more you try to wrestle that bone out of its mouth, the more it fights to hang on. With some of our own stubbornly held positions, we also hold on out of pride and a sense of ownership. Some of us will go to the grave before we let go.

Teasing my clients, I sometimes say that when we get hooked into certain positions, we have lapsed into temporary insanity. I'm only half joking here. If insanity is the loss of contact with reality, then I've certainly been there. Fortunately for you and me, we can find our way back. It requires some maturity to see where we are and how to proceed. But first we must admit that a serious loss of perspective is equivalent to a loss of reality. Extreme thinking creates illusions, maybe delusions, about the way things truly are.

Let's look a closer at extreme thinking. Each stage can cause severe problems. They are also places that can be interrupted with reality-testing; then new options can be considered. The stages of "extreme-thinking warfare" are:

Stage #1: Feeling the first shot of adrenaline. I've already said that the extreme thinker is quick to react. Anger flares. Was the fight precipitated by toothpaste, toilet paper, or spilled jam on the counter? Whatever it is, our emotions have been "hooked" and our more rational nature has taken a coffee break. Now we're reacting with adrenaline; our vision has been restricted and goodwill is slipping away.

Stage #2: Setting up the initial boundary lines of defense. This is basically a well-honed and often-practiced exercise in self-righteousness. Having lost perspective and wanting to defend the *right* way of thinking, we criticize the "stupid" thinking of our mate as we elevate our own position. At this stage a person likes to assert—sometimes with biblical quotes!—that his ideas cannot be challenged because they come straight from on high. You get the point.

Stage #3: Erecting the sturdy bulwarks of blame. As the extreme thinking continues, and in fact escalates, each partner will attack the other and blame their mates for all mutual problems. The finger is always pointing at the other. Listen closely and you will hear, "You did *this*!" and "It's your fault."

Stage #4: Hurling the missiles of shame. Now, believing that she (or he) is right and the other person is wrong, this "true-believer" will sometimes shift to the ultimate weapon of shaming. This cruelest form of attack shifts attention from the other's ideas or actions to spew venom onto the person's essential self. Effective here are name-calling and criticizing the mate's intelligence, character, and motives. Perhaps most unfair are attacks against a partner's family members, who aren't there to defend themselves. Such acts of desperation, which denigrate the very personhood of the other, are not quickly forgiven or forgotten.

Stage #5: Enlisting the agents of depersonal assassination. In any kind of combat, it always helps the troops be able to kill if the enemy soldier can be depersonalized—made to appear as a less-than-human specimen of "evil." (Use your imagination here. Ever accused your spouse of "inhuman" behavior?) Of course, intellectually, we know that it's our *ideas* that are in conflict, not our actual personhood, so attacks that depersonalize help us to attack the other's selfhood without feeling guilty.

Stage #6: Planning for the big, all-out counterattack. We're talking revenge here! It will come, and it will be devastating. Since we are now feeling hurt and wounded, we seek to retaliate, perhaps biding our time until the battle conditions are just right. As in war, we use whatever destructive force we can muster. Not only do we not want to consider another's point of view, we want to humiliate and shut them up. This can be a terribly destructive stage in a relationship.

Stage #7: Maintaining the cold war . . . forever? Finally, not surprisingly, emotional distance develops and widens. Extreme thinking has become set in stone, and a patterned way of relating becomes engrained, with standard attacks and counterattacks. The walls are up and fortified. The home is not a safe shelter. It's cold and dangerous there. Not unlike in childhood, when facing the neighborhood bully we retreat into whatever safety we can find. All intimacy is lost. This pattern of isolation from one another will last forever unless we build a bridge to create new, healthier patterns of communication.

Making Your Home Safe Again

I just took a deep sigh. How about you? It is a tragedy that so much humiliation fills the home, the citadel that was meant to be a healing refuge from the strains of daily life. This is where we should be able to replenish our frayed minds and bodies after toiling away in a hectic society.

Let's move forward and see how we can make our homes that safe place again. After all, that is why you are reading this book. You have had enough of war; you want domestic peace. Why not take the first two steps: *reducing blame and increasing responsibility?*

No More Blame-Throwing!

After the short, sweet honeymoon, we begin to see the warts of our lover. When we see those faults and failures, we consciously or unconsciously want to assign blame. It's as if our marital problems are a legal matter: "Who is right, your Honor? I have proof that I am in the right, and my spouse, here, is in the wrong. Justice must be served!"

Perhaps you have patterns in your marriage where you repeatedly attack one another. You have experienced ambushes to your self-esteem when you least expected it. You have realized that you weren't safe even in your own home, where, more than anywhere else you expect to be safe. In extreme situations, where things were not safe, you may have felt as if you were losing your mind. This is called "crazymaking." Your opinions did not matter. Whenever you expressed your point of view, there was something wrong with it. You felt blamed for everything because your spouse did not have the inner strength to accept responsibility for his or her own "stuff" and, instead, projected it onto you. "Oh, sure, theoretically, I know that I have faults. But, because I am always in search of affirmation, I don't want to hear that something I'm doing disrupts our marriage. I want to talk about what you are doing that's so destructive. Your faults are so obvious. I practically feel like a psychologist because I see so clearly how our marriage would improve if you changed."

Jesus said that we must guard against any tendency to judge others. We are all sinners with warts and faults. "Why do you look at the speck of sawdust in your brother's eye and pay no attention to the plank in your own eye?" (Matthew 7:3) It's easier to blame others while excusing our own shortcomings.

But we must lay down our blame-throwers in this war!

Blamers want to dodge responsibility by pointing a sharp finger at the other person. To protect fragile egos, they look through a magnifying glass at the faults of others while wearing blinders to avoid seeing their own. *The problems are always about the other person!* Oh, if these blamers could understand that this self-serving response only creates fear and division. Ultimately, it diverts them from their goal of saving the marital relationship.

More "Response-able" Responses

Now it's time to look at the positive side of things: There is a way to interrupt destructive patterns so that we can have just the kind of marriage we want—free from power and control tactics and full of loving affirmations. The solution, in a nutshell, is to *take responsibility*. Let me explain with an illustration from a couple who came for counseling some time ago.

Terry and Karla had come in for counseling the same way most come: with too much baggage and almost too late. They were close to a meltdown. Both were ready to call it quits, but they agreed to a plan in which we would work together for eight sessions to see if they could restore any of the bliss they'd enjoyed ten years earlier when they fell in love.

Strategy Step
Try Replacing Blame with Affirmation

Suppose we were to replace our blaming words with affirming ones? What would that be like? It would definitely involve offering *encouragement* and extending *affection*.

What *encouragement* might sound like:

"I know it's going to be hard, but I believe in you."

"What can I do to help you accomplish your goals this week?"

"If anyone can make it, you can, and I'd like to join you in that goal."

"Tomorrow's a new day, and I'm excited to live it with you."

What *affection* might sound like:

"You are so precious to me."

"You mean the world to me. I don't know what I'd do without you."

"I love you so very much."[4]

As with the couples that I've described before in this chapter, both Terry and Karla felt *pushed to extremes*. Hostility and resentment were high. Respect was at a low. Distrust colored everything they said to each other. They felt none of the attraction and affection they'd shared years ago. After so much quarreling and blaming, could they rebuild bonds of love?

We began work by experimenting with some new principles. I reassured and challenged them: "Folks, you do not feel good about one another *not* because there is nothing to feel good about. Rather, you don't feel good because you spend so much time saying destructive things and too little time saying affirming things to one another. You are both starved for affection and affirmations of what matters to you. You want your mate to tell you that your ideas are valid and that you are wonderful just the way you are. To arrive at that place, you will both put aside some tactics that don't work and begin using principles that do work. Instead of automatically *reacting* to situations, usually in old destructive patterns, you can now *respond* using encouragement. While our power is limited, God's is not. Are you game?"

Terry and Karla agreed to change the direction of things so that the love would begin to grow again. It was a decision to practice a new form of *"response-ability"*—that is, the ability to *respond to old patterns with new options*. Let's look closely at a few of these new options that any of us can choose. We'll need them when we're standing on the brink of one of our all-too-familiar marital conflicts.

First, you can always choose the option of taking responsibility for your own behavior, instead of focusing on the behavior of your partner. Because his or her faults are obvious, who better to point them out than you, right?

Wrong!

Unless our partner's behavior directly impacts us, we need to let her live her own life. This principle is based on respect; that is, granting each individual the right to live his or her own life. After all, you have enough to focus on as you apply all the principles for a happy relationship in this book.

If you find that you are being criticized, remember that you don't have to "own" everything your spouse tells you, but you can listen and value your mate's point of view. I like to encourage people to at least consider what part of the feedback might fit. "Chew up the meat and spit out the bones."

Second, you can remember that every human being is fallible. None of us is perfect or without fault. It's important to keep this in perspective. In addition, we all have problems and limitations. So there is no reason for anyone to be self-righteous. Let go of trying to change your spouse, and a freedom will flow through your relationship. Each person needs to be who he or she is without fear of constant criticism.

Terry and Karla were quite flexible with this principle. They had played "the blame game" for years and were now willing to let go of their arrogance to practice seeing the other's point of view. They practiced looking at their own roles in conflicts as opposed to focusing on their partner's role. The more

Strategy Steps

Find the Positive Side

Healthy couples have learned to take what was said or done—something that was discouraging or disheartening in the past—and turn it into something positive, something from which they can learn and grow. Here's a chart to get you started. Insert your mate's negative traits and reframe them into positive perceptions. Once you get the concept, begin practicing turning "negative" aspects into positive perceptions. It's the essence of honoring your spouse.

Negative Trait	Positive Perception
Nosy	He may be overly alert or sociable.
Touchy	She may be very sensitive.
Manipulating	He may be a very resourceful person with creative ideas.
Stingy	She may be very thrifty.
Talkative	He may be very expressive or dynamic.
Flighty	She may be an enthusiastic person with cheerful vitality.
Too serious	He may be very earnest, with strong convictions.
Too bold	She may have strong convictions and standards.
Rigid	He may be well-disciplined, with strong convictions.
Overbearing	She may be a very confident person.
A dreamer	He may be very creative and imaginative.
Too fussy	She may be very organized and efficient.[5]

they practiced this principle, the stronger their marriage became.

Third, you can choose to stop the shaming. Shaming says someone is inadequate, that he or she fails to measure up as a human being. Over time the victim of our shaming words begins feeling defective at the very core of her being.

Karla had been especially angry about Terry's lack of church attendance. She had been using shame as a tool to manipulate him into attending with her. However, she readily acknowledged that it was not working. In fact, since it pushed him away from church, she finally agreed to let his attendance be a matter between him and God. She understood that refusing to shame him would help their marriage as well as his attendance.

Any form of shaming and blaming distracts us from effective problem solving. When I get that tense feeling inside because I'm sitting with a couple who are choosing to attack one another, I often stop the interaction and ask them to listen more closely to what they are doing. I then ask them if they want to keep attacking or start looking for solutions to their problems. Their fighting is a big waste of time, hurts the relationship, and keeps the real issues from being addressed. Quite simply, it is not a good idea.

Fourth, when approaching conflict, you can remember the difference between preferences and ethics. In other words, many issues are a matter of style or preference, not of right or wrong. There are very few absolutes in this world, though you would never know this if you were to listen to the average couple hurling verbal grenades at one another! When we get uptight, we start acting as if winning is everything, regardless of how petty the issue. (Ever had that sinking feeling a day after a fight, wondering why you made such a big deal out of such a trivial matter?) The point is: we can begin to see many of our differences as matters of taste, not as personal attacks on the foundations of our moral framework.

Finally, you can extend forgiveness—over and over again. Jesus tells us that we will be forgiven to the same measure that we forgive. I'm reminded of a couple who struggled to "forgive and forget" many past wounds that came from having been deeply involved in drugs and alcohol. While they'd been freed from the former addictions, they still clung tenaciously to some of the hurts they endured during those times. No amount of discussing the "whys" seemed to relieve the pain they had experienced.

What seemed to help this couple was practicing the principle of "laying it down." They practiced asking God to lift their heavy burden, thanking Him for the spirit of forgiveness they knew that they would receive for their partner. They envisioned a life without hurt and anger and offered those emotions up to God. They then practiced basking in the presence of God, imagining—and celebrating—a life with their spouse that would be filled with trust and joy. While there was no instant cure for the wounds they had experienced, repetitive meditative prayer seemed to be a soothing balm that allowed God to transform sorrow into celebration for the new relationship they experienced today.

I remember when our eldest son began to consistently say that he was sorry for things he had done wrong. It came after a long, adolescent season of blaming others for his actions. Instead of squirming and looking for ways to justify what he had done, he learned to say he was sorry. I melted with pride and fondness for him.

Perhaps you have felt the same way in your marriage or some other relationship. There is something refreshing about "owning your stuff." It frees you up to be genuine and trusting. It produces safety and intimacy.

We are all human and will make mistakes on a daily basis. Come to expect it. Don't be surprised when your partner forgets to do something you have asked him/her to do. You are certainly right to hold your mate accountable, but keep in mind that it is not a life-or-death matter. Things may, and often do, look very different a day later. Keep a clean emotional slate with your partner!

See Dick and Jane Grow Up

Once again, let us imagine how things might be if Dick and Jane began moving from blaming to taking responsibility . . .

Imagine a Heart-Change for Dick

Dick and Linda were able to enjoy a rare evening out without their children, free from responsibilities and distractions. It was refreshing to both, as they were hungry for contact with one another. They'd agreed that they would treat themselves to an evening out at least once a month, and each would take a turn at choosing the activity. They had further agreed that it would be a surprise, and each had to have a good attitude about the event their spouse chose.

So much for well laid plans!

On their way out of the house, Dick asked Linda for directions to "the big event." They chatted comfortably as they drove down the freeway to the appropriate exit.

When Linda directed Dick to the opera house parking lot, he did a double-take. He wondered if it were possible that Linda would take him to something he detested. Surely she wouldn't do that to him!

As they climbed out of the car, Dick asked politely what they would be doing. When she pointed to the opera house, he cringed. He tried to force a smile, but his displeasure was clear. In a moment he was angry and didn't hide it. How would they handle this crisis?

"I thought it might be kind of fun to see a live play. It's not an opera," she said reassuringly. "I know how you feel about those."

"Well, to be honest," Dick said, "I'm not sure about a play, but . . . ." He stopped and chose his words carefully. He didn't want to hurt Linda's feelings and had agreed to be a good sport about whatever she chose to do on the date.

"I know you put a lot of planning into this, and it's one of the few times we have out, so let's give it a try. I like being with you and, well, I might like the play."

Imagine a Heart-Change for Jane

Rushing into the kitchen, Jane grabbed the phone. It was her friend Betsy, wondering if she were free to have a "girl's night out" in Portland.

Jane was excited as she listened about where she and her friends would be staying if she chose to go along. Betsy had outdone herself with making detailed arrangements. She had found a group rate at the downtown Hilton, and knew of a sale nearby at Nordstroms. She had also checked out the movies playing near the hotel.

"So, what do you think?" Betsy asked. "Too good to pass up, huh?"

"Yeah," said Jane. "I can't miss this. You've worked hard to arrange everything. You need to get a life!" Both laughed.

As Jane became caught up in the moment, she noticed Rob looking at her from the dining room. He could sense what was happening. At first she turned her head to avoid his critical look. Then she paused and asked Betsy if she could call her right back.

"You overheard what's happening," Jane said softly. "I have an opportunity to go to town with the girls next weekend. But if you think I shouldn't go, I won't."

"It's not what I think that's important," Rob said. "Of course I'm concerned about your being with them and maybe feeding the spending urge. What do you think?"

"I think I'd die to go and be with them," Jane said slowly. She walked over to the window and looked at the fir trees and creek that ran behind their home.

"But," she said, with her voice trailing off, "I know it wouldn't be good for me. I have to tackle this thing head on. Desire's okay but it needs to be attached to the right things.

"I hate working on this stuff."

Think and Discuss

1. Of the issues discussed in this chapter, which are most relevant to your own situation these days?

2. Are you willing to take "response-ability" for change in these areas? What would that look like?

3. List some goals for your behavior in your marital relationship.

4. Consider an issue that you would be willing to hold up in prayer with your spouse. Envision the situation already healed by God!

Implementing Your "Marriage Makeover" Plan

Note: Each spouse should take time, in advance, to jot his or her responses to these questions on a separate sheet of paper before coming together for sharing and discussion.

"Growing Up" Step #3:
Moving from Blame to Responsibility

Key task: *Learn the reasons for, and methods of, unfair attacking—and avoid them at all costs.*

1. Go back to the beginning of this chapter and analyze the interactions between the couples. Choose a statement made by one of the spouses. Replace or rewrite it in a way that could open the door for a new direction in the conversation. (In other words, what could this person have said that would have reduced the tension and blame-throwing?) Jot your statement here:

_____

_____

_____

2. When do you typically feel a need to attack? When does your spouse feel this need? Do some further thinking about this:

- *The typical circumstances before an attack:*

- *The most likely time(s) of day:*

- *The conversational patterns that begin to develop, preceding the attack:*

3. After doing the analysis in #2 above, work with your spouse on answering:

• *Where could we begin to step in when we see these patterns developing and leading to a fight?*

• *What could we change about the circumstances—or our attitudes—that would turn the conversation in a more productive direction?*

4. Think about your attitudes for a moment.

• *When have I been most guilty of extreme thinking with my spouse? An example is:*

• *When has my spouse been most guilty of extreme thinking? An example is:*

5. Which types of unfair fighting methods do we often use?

6. In what creative way could we safely remind one another that one of us is slipping into unfairness? (Try to come up with a creative reminder—a certain word to say during an argument? Holding up a hand? Walking to a designated place in the house?) Write down your ideas here:

4 Taking All the Toys

*T*hat *is my toy," said Jane.*
"No," said Dick. "That is mine!"
Take, Jane. Take it now!

The phone rang just as Dick walked in the door from work. Linda would not be back from school for another hour.

"Hello."

"Hey, whatcha doing, Dick?" came the voice on the line. "This is Jim, and a bunch of us are going out for a quick bike ride this evening before it gets dark. Are you up for it?"

"Sounds great. Where are you going?"

"We're meeting at my place in half an hour and then heading up to the Spencer Creek trail. Can you be here?"

"I'll be there. See you then."

As soon as Dick hung up the phone, he began preparing for the ride. Then it hit him. He had agreed to spend more time with Linda. . . .

* * * * * *

Jane wasn't out riding mountain bikes; her playground was the mall. Her toys were her clothes. But her preoccupation with looking good had choked her checking account, as well as her judgment.

Rob pleaded with her to spend less time and money at the malls and more time with him. "I feel like I'm taking second or third place in your life, Jane," he'd said one evening after a bitter squabble.

When she came back at him with a sarcastic dig, all he could think was: *I'm losing her—one dollar at a time.*

Of course, Rob knew he'd been taking more than he had given. Less transparent than Jane's self-flaunting was Rob's determination to guard his emotions at all costs. He'd helped create the distance between them. He'd been more critical than affirming. As a result, his emotional "bank account" with Jane was severely overdrawn.

Now that the overdrafts were coming in the mail, what could Rob do?

The Painful Symtoms of Our "Taking Disease"

If our goal is to develop a healthy marriage, then we're admitting from the start that there's some "sickness" in the relationship. It's true of most couples. But the difference between those who move on to health and those who flounder in their relational "disease" is that some couples never acknowledge that *there are no shortcuts to marital bliss.*

I recall a time when I raised chickens and decided to try my hand at incubating the eggs. I had about thirty eggs, turning them over daily in the incubator. Constantly monitoring the heat and humidity, I could see the embryos growing; however, I just couldn't contain my excitement and decided to help those little ones obtain a head start. As they began to peck their way out of their shells in a seemingly tortuous ordeal, I selected one faltering chick and chipped away at its shell, helping it escape from captivity.

I expected that chick to come out and do everything but whistle Dixie. That did not happen! My young companion not only didn't whistle but in a few short moments it died. After repeating my rescue attempt another time or two, with similar results, I realized that my "assistance" turned out to be a struggling chick's death knell. It was a memorable lesson in not taking shortcuts.

In marital growth, avoiding shortcuts means facing our symptoms squarely, and then looking at our choices for influencing the future prognosis. That is the plan of this chapter. First, we'll review key symptoms of a diseased marriage—spouses who (1) demand immediate gratification; (2) fear not having enough; and (3) dread facing their inner emptiness. To clarify the nature of each of these symptoms, we'll be asking the kind of question a "marriage doctor" (like me!) might put to each spouse in counseling. Now for those symptoms.

We "Swell Up" with a Demand for Immediacy

• *Question: Are you sickened by a manipulative cycle of blaming, defending, attacking . . . and blaming?* There are no shortcuts, remember? But it seems that many of us demand immediate gratification of every desire, no matter what the cost to our spouse. In effect we have elected to drop out of Relationship Skills 101 and hope that we can use charm and manipulation to get our way in this world. Unfortunately, in the arena of marriage, manipulation has the same impact as two ticks continually sucking blood out of one another. Soon both run out of blood and die.

Let's take a look at Jerry and Pat. At puberty they were Relationship School dropouts. Like many other young people, they expected others to give to them. Not unlike Narcissus in the Greek myth, who fell in love with his own mirrored image, both Jerry and Pat pursued their self-centered pleasures. After they married, each expected the other to play the role of giver and pleaser.

In psychological terms, their immature behavior would be called egocentric and narcissistic. Impulsive, they seemed to believe that they should be able to take and take until it killed their mate. Sadly, they demonstrated what happens when two adults are really two-year-olds at heart.

Problems appeared almost as soon as the wedding cake disappeared. Yet neither Jerry nor Pat noticed exactly what was happening: that neither could tolerate frustration and each had to have what "I want"—*now.* Instead of focusing on *maturing their style of relating,* they obsessed on *obtaining their desires of the moment.* He would accuse her of being grouchy for no reason. She would blame him for various perceived infractions. And so it went, on and on, creating a festering cycle of blaming, defending, attacking, and more blaming. No wonder their relationship began falling apart!

The most important problem in Jerry and Pat's relationship was that each expected the other to fix things so that they would be instantly gratified. Each was an expert at taking, but neither of them did well at giving. Neither spent the time and energy necessary to really try to understand the other partner's needs. Stephen Covey, in his bestselling book *The Seven Habits of Highly Effective People,* correctly says that we must first seek to understand before seeking to be understood. This takes time, and lots of it. But what a wonderful world it would be if we all practiced this principle of maturity!

Danger Here!

The Terrible Results of Neglect

When we fail to become lovingly involved with our spouse at the point of that person's need, a complex and painful chain reaction may be set in motion. For example:

• If a spouse is not properly appreciated, he may struggle with feelings of insignificance.

• If a spouse does not receive support, she may feel overwhelmed and hopeless.

• If a spouse is not encouraged, he may grow weary and give up.

• If a spouse fails to receive comfort for her emotional hurts, inner healing can be seriously hindered.

• If a spouse is not granted sufficient attention, he may lose a sense of being important to others.

• If a spouse does not receive acceptance, she may have difficulty grasping her worth in God's eyes.

• If a spouse does not receive sufficient affection, she may feel unloved and unlovable.

• If a spouse does not receive respect, he may feel ignored and unimportant.

• If a spouse does not sense security in the relationship, she may be paralyzed by fear and distrust.

• If a spouse does not receive approval, his sense of value may be diminished.[1]

We Become Infected with a Fear of Scarcity

• *Question: Are you overly concerned about not be getting your "fair share"?* Does your behavior reveals that at the core you believe we live in a world of too little, that there is not enough to go around? Even though the Scriptures make it clear that our Creator provided our world with great abundance, we too often act as if ours is a world of scarcity.

The disease of hoarding and collecting is so insidious that many do not see it developing. We see ourselves as "normal" and simply doing what we see all of our contemporaries doing. We encourage single-minded ambition as one aspect of "being the best we can be." After all, our world unquestionably values possessing, collecting, and accumulating as ends in themselves. At the end of life, those with the most toys "win."

I recall an example of this possessing and hoarding behavior by our son when he was two years old. After a particularly gift-filled birthday (with his parents absentmindedly reinforcing many of the values we didn't really want reinforced), when it came time to share his new wealth with his cousins, he let out an outraged scream, "Toys R' Mine!" There was no question in his mind as to who owned these toys. They were not for the common good. Certainly they were not for sharing, whatever that meant. His world was small, and he was perfectly content to hang on to his booty for dear life. Okay, Mom and Dad. Time to work on growing a civilized boy! It became one of our primary passions for the next sixteen years.

The truth of the matter is that our sons learned some of this behavior from their father. Oh, I was good at sharing my baseball mitt and bat that were tucked away in the corner of the garage. The kids didn't even need to ask permission to use those things, I would gallantly say. I was a big boy and knew how to share.

Or did I?

What about when they wanted to pluck my new guitar? Or borrow my CB radios? Or use the computer without my watching their every move?

> ## Self-Check
> ### How Territorial Are You?
>
> Jot your responses to each of the questions below, and then make an appointment to discuss them with your spouse. Together, decide on what changes are needed.
>
> Consider which of your possessions are not to be shared. What makes them so precious?
>
> Are all of your precious things necessary to you? To which might you be overly attached?
>
> Think about how you were raised in your family of origin. What attitudes in your parents might have contributed to a fear of scarcity in you today?

Actually, my kids will tell you that I can hang on pretty tightly to my "toys" too. They know when to walk softly around something that I consider valuable. The "little boy" is still alive and well inside and comes out screaming at unexpected times. And if you think such childish symptoms don't create more than a few health problems in our marriage, then think again.

See Dick play with his toys.

Look! Here comes Jane.

"Go away," says Dick. "Go now."

We Succumb to Futility

• *Question: Are you still trying to fill that hole in your soul?* So, how do we explain this ungenerous regression into the "terrible twos," where everything you have is mine, and everything I have is mine also? Why is it we still don't want to share after we've grown up? What happened to Dick and Jane? Didn't they grow up sharing their toys and then live happily ever after? Tell me it's so!

> ## Partnering Point
>
> People are reaching the top, using all of their means to get money, power, and glory—and then self-destruct. Perhaps they never wanted success in the first place, or didn't like what they saw when they finally achieved it. Perhaps success and excess are so inextricably linked that to achieve one is to invite the other.[2]

No, our social and moral development keeps hitting the potholes of life. Surprisingly, one of the culprits creating the havoc of self-centeredness, in all its varied forms, is *low self-esteem*. Yes, I know this term has been overused and means different things to different people. Self-esteem, or lack thereof, gets the blame for everything from school misbehavior to the world economic crisis. I'm not taking it that far, but consider some ideas with me.

Self-esteem suggests that we'll feel good about ourselves if we just learn to accept who we are, warts and all. In addition, we'll know that things will work out and that there are enough opportunities to go around. We can appreciate what we have, and, believe it or not, can even rejoice in the good fortunes of others. (Okay, so that is a bit advanced for most of us!)

Yet, most of us have bruises and scars from hurtful experiences that have left us with feelings of inadequacy, of not having or *being* enough. This sense of *not enough* drives us to try to take far beyond what is needed for our happiness. It's as if we think we can fill these inadequacy chuckholes of emptiness by collecting things, degrees, conquests, and other socially approved trophies. Sadly, few of us have any idea of how to cope with these troubling feelings. We want to fill our emptiness, this "hole in our soul," and our sense of deficiency crazily propels us toward self-destruction. It's as if we say to ourselves, "Watch out! Here comes a bad feeling. Hurry. Get rid of it. Do something!"

In the nineties it was as if there were a plague of low self-esteem; people became insatiable—hoarding, grabbing, taking, all the while secretly dreading the futility of trying to engineer their happiness accumulating material things.

In their search to alter a "bad mood" or find an elusive euphoria, some even in this new millennium pursue the addictions that I talked about in chapter 2—drugs, alcohol, sex, work, shopping, eating, gambling, to name a few. Others have taken up an obsessive hoarding that fails to satisfy, and, perhaps worse, isolates them from those they love.

Whatever our own choice of "escape," the drives become stronger as we become more desperate to satisfy the inner cravings. Thus, the addictive process gains momentum.

What makes this struggle all the more pathetic is that the hole in our soul is actually a "God-shaped vacuum," as Blaise Pascal put it. This vacuum can only be filled by God. Our answer lies in the words of the old hymn, "nothing satisfies like Jesus." Without Him it is like continually seeking water from an empty well, never realizing that the well is empty—and never fully understanding why we remain parched. We try to bolster our flagging self-esteem with trivialities, when what is needed is a relationship with the Creator of the Universe.

The LIKELY Prognosis—When Taking Takes Over

As our compulsive behaviors grow and we continue our attitude of scarcity and taking, the feelings of insecurity are not addressed. We cannot get enough of our "fix," whatever that is, while the disease remains unhealed. This leads to two predictable, though vastly differing, outcomes. One possible outcome is deadness—a deepening coldness and insensitivity in the marriage. But there is another possibility, one that leads to life and an increasing vitality, warmth, and renewed spirit of adventure. The choice is ours.

Danger Here!
When Enough Is Enough

Beware! Here are four mechanisms that make people feel it's just too hard to get their needs met in the relationship:

1. *"I can do whatever I want, right?"* Your partner is making unilateral moves—doing what he wants when he wants it, by himself, without talking to you about it.

2. *"It's such an ordeal talking about the littlest thing."* Negotiating solutions together has become virtually impossible because: You feel furious and deprived or exhausted and overwhelmed. OR: You're afraid of being attacked, because your partner's a "historian" and hooks everything you bring up into the past or because you're constantly criticized when you have a need. OR: You're afraid of conflict and struggle, because every single negotiation in the past has ended in disaster.

3. *"You never do what you say you're going to do."* This is where the issue of trust comes up in relationships. When people make agreements and then break them, the relationship is not only a place of fighting and deprivation, it's a place of betrayal.

4. *"We're very polite with each other."* This is what happens to people in a relationship when they're furious and exhausted from pointless fighting, broken agreements, and unmet needs. But now there's no fighting; there's just despair.[3]

Possibility #1: A lifetime of deadly codependency. One of the hallmarks of maturity is the ability to tolerate pain or discomfort. Yet in our search for "the good feeling," most of us have about a two-minute or less threshold for

Technical Talk
Co-What?

There are many ways to define codependency. But here is a good, broad explanation:

Codependence is a disease of lost selfhood....We become codependent when we turn our responsibility for our life and happiness over to our ego (our false self) and to other people. Codependents become so preoccupied with others that they neglect their true self—who they really are....When we focus so much *outside* of ourselves we lose touch with what is *inside* of us: our beliefs, thoughts, feelings, decisions, choices, experiences, wants, needs, sensations, intuitions, unconscious experiences, and even indicators of our physical functioning, such as heart rate and respiratory rate....

Codependence is the most common of all addictions: the addiction to looking elsewhere....The "elsewhere" may be people, places, things, behaviors or experiences. Whatever it is, we may neglect our own selves for it.[4]

pain or discomfort before we start screaming. One way we deal with our discomforts is to *look to our partners to fix us*. We are behaving *co-dependently* when we believe that it is the other person's responsibility to make us feel good. If we get used to relating to our spouse this way, then we will set up a pattern of relating that is decidedly "sick."

In my work with couples I often find traits of codependency. Such was the case with Ben and Margaret. This middle-age couple really struggled with conflict. It seemed that neither could stand the least hint of criticism. It was as if both wore a sticker on their forehead saying, "If you criticize me, then you don't love me." In this kind of environment neither felt free to voice their genuine complaints. Doing so would be tantamount to denying their love for one another!

Fragile egos in tow, Ben and Margaret grew more and more distant from one another. Like two porcupines trying to dance, they could not seem to make contact without injuring the other. Their only solution, they reasoned, was to part company because they realized that their dance was not working. Thankfully, through counseling they did learn to receive complaints without catastrophizing. In time they were also able to "see" that constructive conflict helped clear the air and make room for intimacy.

It's terribly burdensome to a marriage when one mate cannot feel good unless the other mate behaves in a certain way. For example, if one mate demands that the other always be available by phone or in person at any time, or if one holds the other responsible for lost or misplaced items, or if one mate

Self Check
Are You Codependent

If you suspect you may have codependent tendencies or that there may be issues of codependency in your marriage, take the following test. Check the statements that are true about your life.

____ I can't stand to be alone.

____ I am a perfectionist.

____ I feel desperate when I cannot gain the approval of others.

____ I find myself making decisions based on how they will affect others and rarely consider myself.

____ Many times I feel obsessed by a need for total order in my life.

____ I put work first, above everything else.

____ I find myself adjusting to my spouse's need rather than communicating my feelings.

____ I do not experience anger.

____ I overeat often.

____ I am constantly wondering what other people think of me.

____ I cover up my feelings so others won't realize what I really think.

____ I am afraid that if others really knew me they would not like me.

____ I am constantly trying to figure how to stay ahead in my relationships.

____ I cover up my feelings of self-doubt with drug or alcohol use.

____ I can't say no when I am asked to do a favor or serve on a committee.

____ When I begin to feel sad or angry I go shopping, work harder, or eat.

____ I tell myself it shouldn't hurt so much when others let me down.

____ I often feel I need to change the way other people behave.

____ I need everyone to be happy with me so that I can feel good about myself.

____ I need others to be strong for me without requiring anything from me in return.

If you checked three or more statements, then there are probably issues of codependency operating in you. The more issues you checked, the greater your need for dealing with the issues and tendencies. Why not seek counseling, so you can examine and resolve these issues and break the cycle?[5]

transfers his or her own insecurity onto the partner and the partner accepts it. All of these needs represent codependence but, actually, the "dependent" person gives away a tremendous amount of power. Why? Because the focus of self-control is placed outside of herself. Because when we're codependent, *we need the other person to act in a certain way for us to feel better.*

In other words, if we ask someone else to take responsibility for our feelings or actions, we lose "self" control. Then, as we suffer a loss of personal power, we feel drained. It's as if we've flushed our self-esteem down a huge suction pipe.

Now my point in this whole discussion is this: Codependency can be a very subtle form of "taking." We can be very childlike as we "demand" that our spouse give us something that we should create for ourselves, or more importantly, find in our relationship to God.

But remember, I'm not talking about asking for things from a partner that are legitimate, such as respect, affection, or the willingness to listen with the heart. What I am talking about is wrongly demanding that our spouse feed us in a caretaking way. When we want our spouse constantly to make us feel better or to solve all of our problems, we ask too much.

There are many other ways that we become self-absorbed in a marriage and fail to meet the legitimate needs of our spouse while fully expecting that our desires will be fulfilled. If we maintain a childish notion that *"you are here to meet my needs,"* an imbalance seeps in that creates a deadening marital prognosis.

But there is hope—another blessed possibility—when we find the "taking mentality" taking over our marriage.

Possibility #2: The healing potential of complete breakdown. Sometimes we come to the end of our resources as we try to fix our lives or mend the precious relationships that lay broken around us. At those times, we can sink lower into defeat. Or we can let the breakdown itself become the means to a powerful breakthrough.

I know of a millionaire couple who lived in the fast lane and seemed to enjoy every minute of it. Wielding great power and influence, they were envied far and wide. They had the Midas touch, in business and in social skills.

All of this became meaningless to them, however, when they found that they could create everything but the precious gift of a child. For years they sought out the best doctors, consulted fertility specialists, and even experimented with several nontraditional methods to produce a baby. It all proved futile. In the end, their power and money could not buy the gift of life.

Just as this husband and wife began resigning themselves to a life without children she unexpectedly became pregnant. Needless to say, they were ecstatic. Had God heard their earnest, beseeching cries at last? Up from the valley of despair, they soared to the heights of ecstasy.

Not long into their celebration, though, they were forced back to earth by the words of their Beverly Hills obstetrician. "I'm afraid I have bad news. Your child will be born with a genetic defect that will handicap him for life." As he explained it all in devastating detail, they felt their hopes and dreams quickly melting away.

They were crushed. They were angry.

They went through weeks of agony about whether to end the pregnancy. Many of their friends told them to abort and try again. Something deep within, however, said this was not the right thing to do. They decided to deliver.

What happened during the next few years was nothing short of miraculous. Their child was challenged in many ways, causing Mom and Dad to give of themselves beyond any reasonable limits. They would never know what it was like to have a "normal" child, but the transformation in them was worth it. Let's listen to them tell it.

"At first we kept asking why this happened to us. What had we done to deserve this tragedy? But we learned to love Terrel more than we ever imagined. We give him the credit for altering our lives and giving God a chance to change us. We were so self-centered, empty, and bitter. We were slowly dying in our own way. Terrel gave us our life back. He gave us a chance to give back to someone who could only love us back. All he could do was love. And what we needed most was love."

The breakdown can be a good thing, especially when we finally figure out that IT is not working—whatever our chosen "fix" may be. This is when we are forced to change. This is when we see that having more does nothing to satisfy our yearning for meaning, and cannot overcome our feelings of inadequacy.

It's so inspiring to talk with someone who has come through such a blessed meltdown. Feeling compelled to take some time off, to get away from the rat race, they often come back with an entirely renewed perspective. While most of us will find a thousand reasons never to pull ourselves out of the daily grind, those who do tell us the experience is invaluable.

If you are clearly heading for a breakdown in your marriage, please approach it with some sense of anticipation. I know that you may still feel depressed and fearful at the same time. But remember that there is a kernel of life waiting to blossom in the seemingly dead seeds of marital disharmony. You need not choose the path of codependency when "taking" has taken over. You can make a turn for the better.

You can let your losses and heartaches move you up onto a new plain where your own ability to cope finally gives way to God's abilities to heal. As you loosen your grip on controlling your own circumstances, you'll open up spaces of hurt, frustration, and sadness before the Lord. As you find that this is "safe" with God—that He can fill those hungry spaces with healing love—you will begin, tentatively, to open up to your spouse as well. The new level of give-and-take will move you closer together. It will take time; you may need a counselor to help you. But enthusiasm and zest will return. The sunsets will be majestic again, birds will sing their rhapsodies, and your partner will be absolutely adorable.

Yes, you will be *present* again and able to see with new eyes. After all, *"There can be no breakthrough without a breakdown."*

See Dick and Jane Grow Up

Our attitudes about giving and taking, developed over many years, will not change instantly. However, it's okay to "fake it until you make it," starting slowly to understand the importance of shifting our focus from taking to giving.

Are you ready to make that shift? There is something quite marvelous about letting go of our egos enough to care at least as much about others as we care about ourselves. Often this maturity is gained through years of experience. In addition to whatever books they may have read, mature persons have seen what really works, and what does not. Mature individuals have also experienced many joys, sorrows, and hardships. They may have had the "breakdown" that causes them to reexamine everything in their lives, including their beliefs. They may have had a profound spiritual experience, which, if only briefly, permitted them to see through "spiritual eyes" rather than through ego-oriented ones. It is quite likely that you are such a person. Perhaps you've tried a variety of paths and are ready for a more authentic one.

Dick and Jane, with Linda and Rob, are clearly on that path.

Imagine a Heart-Change in Dick . . .

Linda has been trying to get Dick's attention with varying degrees of success. However, while she wants his attention she has not fully realized her own contribution to their problems. While she has complained about his unavailability, she has been preoccupied with her own activities. She, in a sense, has been guilty of the very thing for which she has criticized Dick.

One evening Linda approached Dick in a new way. Instead of attacking him for his outdoor interests, she decided to explore what activities they might do together. She surmised that maybe he wasn't avoiding her as much as he was filling up his time because she was unavailable.

"Dick," Linda said softly. "What would you think about us taking sailing lessons this summer? Neither of us have done that before, but do you think it would be fun to try?"

"I've always thought sailing would be a blast," Dick said, smiling. "I know we've been doing our own thing a lot. But maybe this would be something we'd both like."

"Well," Linda continued. "Since that idea went so well, I'd like to run another thought by you. What would you think of us going together on a short-term mission trip with the church? I've been thinking about us giving something back to others, and it would be a way for us to do something meaningful together too. What do you think?"

"Not exactly my cup of tea," Dick said. "But I don't see how it could hurt me. I guess I'd like to give something back too. . . ."

Imagine a Heart-Change in Jane . . .

Rob walked through the back door one sultry evening in late summer. He was irritable and edgy. His work as a newly minted civil engineer was stressful. He felt a pressure to keep up with the veterans, though clearly he did not have their experience.

As soon as he walked in the door and noticed shopping bags on the couch, he jumped to conclusions.

"What are all these bags?" he barked.

"Rob," Jane said softly. "Settle down. They aren't what you think. They're some gifts for your parent's anniversary. I told you that I'm working on my spending, and I'm serious about it. What's the matter with you?"

"Sorry," Rob said. "I had kind of a rough day and I'm taking it out on you. I've seen a change in you and know that you're trying to be sensitive about our issues with money."

"You know, Rob," Jane continued. "It would help me a lot if you could learn to trust me and talk to me about your concerns rather than let them build up inside. I wonder if you build up resentment and then it leaks out at the wrong times? I mean, you can ask me every once in a while how I'm doing with the money, you know."

Rob looked at her for a moment. "I suppose you're right," he said. "I will try to be more direct and upfront about my feelings."

"That sounds good to me," Jane said softly. "I want to help you with your stress about work too. The more we can give to each other the better off we'll be, right? Let's share our struggles more so we can look for ways to solve them together."

Think and Discuss

1. What things does your spouse expect from you? In your opinion, are his or her expectations realistic? Why?

2. Do you give as much as take in your marriage? Explain.

3. What lessons do you suppose you are meant to learn in your marriage?

4. Have you ever been accused of hoarding? What are the areas of your life where you hold on too tightly to things or people?

5. In what ways do you give generously to others?

6. Do you have any problems with codependence? What first steps could you take to begin moving out of codependency?

Implementing Your "Marriage Makeover" Plan

Note: Each spouse should take time, in advance, to jot his or her responses to these questions on a separate sheet of paper before coming together for sharing and discussion.

"Growing Up" Step #4:
Moving from Taking to Giving

Key task: *Look deep within yourself to confront "emptiness" and codependent patterns of relating.*

1. Look again at the chapter-opening vignettes.

• *If you were Dick, how would you have handled the phone call?*

• *If you were Jane, how would you have answered Rob's remark about being "second or third place" in your life?*

2. Think about the possibility of a "Taking Disease" in your life. Consider:

• *When it comes to needing immediate gratification, I'd say . . .*

1_____2_____3_____4_____5
Gotta have   I'm always
everything right   willing to
NOW!   wait and wait.

Possible reasons for my attitude (consider any family-of-origin situations or events):

• When it comes to fearing "there won't be enough," I'd say . . .

1_____2_____3_____4_____5
Gotta get   No worries!
my share,   The Lord
no matter what.   will supply

Possible reasons for my attitude:

• *When it comes to facing "emptiness" inside . . .*

1_____2_____3_____4_____5

I'm so needy!   I feel content
So hungry . . .   and so at
for *what?*   peace within.

Possible reasons for my attitude:

3. Look again at the "Are You Codependent?" self-test. Together, think:

• *How codependent am I? (Name 3 key areas on the test.)*

_____   _____   _____

• *How codependent is my spouse? (Name 3 key areas on the test.)*

_____   _____   _____

• *How has codependency affected our relationship over the years? (Be specific. Listen closely to your spouse's view of things.)*

• *What new ways of relating are open to us? What is a first small step that each of us could take toward freedom?*

Part 2 The Solution

(See Dick and Jane . . . Growing Up!)

5 Trying to Talk

*D*ick *will not talk.*
Jane will not talk.
See Dick and Jane looking sad!

"Say, what's the deal with sex lately?" Dick said angrily. "It seems the bedroom has been off limits. Are you trying to punish me for something? Because if you are, I think it's a pretty rotten thing to do. What gives?"

"There's nothing wrong," Linda replied curtly. "Just don't push me for it so often. Sometimes it seems like it's the only thing on your mind. I need a little space."

"Space! You haven't touched me in a month. Any more space and I'll be living in the next state. Are you having an affair? Because if that's what you want to do, say the word and we'll separate."

"Don't be ridiculous!" she shouted. "That's the last thing I want. I told you. I don't want you pawing me—or pouting when you don't get your way."

Dick stormed toward the door and gave it a big *slam!* on his way out.

******

Jane was only half-listening to the Sunday sermon. As she glanced around the church she noticed all the women and their beautiful clothes. *Sally sure looks good this morning. And there's Wanda—with a new dress . . .*

Comparisons.

Jane could secretly admit that, for her, comparing was a problem. But it was hard to talk about openly. Though she was often complimented, she never felt as if she measured up.

On the ride home she was unusually quiet.

"What's up?" Rob asked.

"Oh, nothing."

Rob immediately became irritated with her tone, feeling as if he might have done something wrong. "Did I say something to make you mad again?" he said.

"Look," Jane said impatiently. "Why don't you just leave me alone? This is not about you. It's some of my old issues. Just back off."

"Wow," Rob said. "If this isn't about me how about if you lighten up a little?"

"Yeah," Jane snapped. "Whatever."

They rode home in silence, watching the miles pass by.

But not enjoying the scenery.

The Fearful Power of Silence

Think about the power of words for a moment. Simple words can convey volumes. They can, over time, build us up and help us to feel secure. Used critically and harshly, words can blindside us and bring us to our knees.

We all have a basic need for acceptance and love, and it is absolutely critical that these things *be verbalized* by our spouse. Without this we fail to thrive. Hungry for verbalized acceptance, we search for it like a lion hunts for food. Yet when conversations like the ones above arise day after day, a relational distance develops. The partners erect barriers of self-protection to maintain some semblance of self-esteem. Eventually, the sound of silence begins to drown out the sweet tones of love.

Get to Know These Sad, Silent Faces!

Yes, silence can do significant damage to a relationship. I'm not saying there shouldn't be "spaces in our togetherness," as one writer put it; rather, we're talking about the silences that squelch intimacy. If we could put faces on the kinds of silence that arise in a marriage, we'd find their personalities to be quite varied and "creative," with numerous effects. Let's look at a few of them and their characteristics. We'll want to be ready to confront them when they raise their unsightly visages in our own marriages.

• *The practiced pucker of the Pouter.* If there's one form of immaturity that seems to pervade adult communication styles, it's pouting. Who, exactly, is the pouter, and why is she so resistant to change? (I use the pronoun "she" here, but men can be accomplished pouters, as well.) Our pouter isn't much different from your daughter or granddaughter when she didn't get the toys she wanted during the latest mall excursion. She had her heart set on that new doll, and when she didn't get it, she let you know about it—again and again. You see, disappointment isn't enjoyable; in fact, it can be downright frustrating.

All of us can relate to little Susie and her desire for the doll. We've all wanted our toys and had our hopes dashed by the cold splash of reality. The kicker here is that as we mature, to some degree or another, we learn to moderate our hopes and expectations and to manage our disappointments. Yes, I did say "to one degree or another." In other words, who said we would, indeed, learn to manage our expectations? We may never have grown up in this area, thus bringing our childhood pouting right into married life.

And pouting is effective! Quicker than anything, it brings our spouses to their knees (think of Jane's pouting on the way home from church). With this powerful "communication tool," we can make others feel guilty, all the while maintaining a secret sense of superiority. With all of these benefits, why would we ever want to advance on the emotional scale of maturity?

But wouldn't we want to change if we could move beyond pouting to find better ways to get our needs met and find happiness? Compare the solution to the use of fire. Fire can hurt us if we touch it directly, just as raw anger can produce a lot of pain. But hiding a fire does no good. If it is "released" wisely, and used within controlled boundaries, it generates a greatly appreciated warmth.

Similarly, with our anger and frustration, it does no good to attempt squelching it, since it will either *explode* or *implode*. Our exploding anger will destroy those around us in a fit of rage or other overtly destructive acts (see the Rageaholic below). Letting it implode means we turn our anger inside and attack our own selves. Then we may pout, letting a little bit of "steam" show through, but mostly we rage against ourselves, and develop at best a nasty attitude and at worst some serious physical symptoms, ranging from dyspeptic digestion or headaches to heart disease.

In other words, the "fire" of being direct with our partners by letting them know our frustrated feelings *while under control*, can show them that we care enough about the relationship to be real with them. This also gives our spouse the opportunity to respond to our hurts and assist in healing them. Together, as a team, we can move forward into healing past wounds. Released from neurotically diverted energies, we can move into being creative, productive, and free

Technical Talk

Throw the Switch!

Ronald E. Smith, Ph.D., director of the Stress Management Training Program in the Department of Psychology at the University of Washington, describes what he has labeled the "ABCs of emotion."

Our emotional reactions, he writes, are the result of our *interpretation* of a situation. He diagrams it like this:

situation (A) leads to

self-statement (B) which leads to

emotional reaction (C)

The ABC concept of emotion, according to Dr. Smith, helps us understand how two people can *experience* the exact same situation and have two different reactions to it. Since B, the self-statement, is equally weighted in this diagram to each of the other parts, A and C, we see that we can change our experience of a situation merely by changing our internal self-statement about it.

This is a skill any of us can learn, and would be especially useful for Pouters and Depressives. We simply "throw the switch" on our self-statements![1]

human beings. Giving up our outdated pouting tool in favor of more sophisticated techniques is a no-brainer in the economics of adult communication and emotional well-being.

One word of caution, however: Giving up our outdated methods may leave us feeling vulnerable for a while. We may want a fig leaf in a world that, at first, appears to be a jungle. It will take time to learn the new, advanced techniques of openness. You can do it!

• *The countenance of the Onerous Introvert.* A little less manipulative, but nonetheless troublesome, is the onerous introvert. I'm not making a value judgment about introverts and extroverts; God made all kinds, and there is not a "right one." But there are some introverts—many of them men—who, although uncomfortable with their introversion, have chosen not only to remain in their ruts but have decorated them with bigscreen TVs with remote controls. Where do you imagine that puts the spouses?

There are a group of men out there, probably 20 million of them, who are more comfortable living in their own inner worlds than interacting with their wives. Yes, they still want to be in a relationship, but they don't want to exert any expressive energy. They're fully capable of learning to share their feelings and carry on delightful conversations; it's just too much trouble. Subsequently, their wives carry the burden of initiating conversation, begging to be listened to, arranging the dinner dates, and generally humiliating themselves for a tightly rationed morsel of love and attention. Do you wonder why such wives are resentful and resort to withholding affection?

Of course, the standard excuse here is: "That's just the way I am!" Yet this is altogether untrue and manipulative. While Sigmund Freud may have considered anyone over thirty to be unchangeable, those days are gone, and so are many of his ideas. It's never too late to change, and we are never too old, as demonstrated by one of my recent clients, named Alan. This eighty-five-year-old man wanted to learn how to communicate more effectively with his eighty-three-year-old wife. He had a sharp wit and intuitively knew that he could have a more meaningful relationship if he put his mind to it. After all, he surmised, he'd been effective at everything else he'd ever undertaken. Why should learning how to listen, respect the other's point of view, and share his feelings be all that much different?

Sadly, Alan is not Mr. Typical. Yet the onerous introverted man can change if he wishes to do so. Do not accept his manipulative position that he is shaped into a mold and cannot break out. He can get out the same way any of us accomplish change: with effort, humility, and focus.

• *The maddening mug of the Depressive.* Another face of silence that hinders marital communication looks almost totally expressionless. This face shows to the world the rigidity of features that comes from suppressed emotion, usually "stuffed" anger. Like throwing a wet blanket on the hot coals of intimacy, depression not only causes the sufferer problems but befuddles the partner as well. It's as if your mate is drowning in a sea of sadness, and you throw out a lifeline only to see it sink right next to her. As your exasperation mounts, you try not to scream, "Just grab the rope, doggone it!"

The Depressive is a second cousin to the Onerous Introvert. Both, you see, are uncomfortable in their particular plight, but usually will not do what needs to be done to become more effective communicators. The Depressives, I must admit, often come by their problems honestly, and they have my empathy. Depression is nothing I'd wish on even my enemy.

Of course, true, clinical depression is a legitimate disease that requires medical treatment. But here I'm mostly referring to a kind of self-imposed self-pity that chooses to view every aspect of life through mud-colored glasses. It's a learned habit practiced over the years by the man or woman who purposely chooses not to confront certain negative thought patterns. In these cases, it's more comfortable to stay helpless.

True depression, though, is effectively treatable more than 90 percent of the time. So there is no reason to suffer alone unless you've become accustomed to that lifestyle and, for self-serving reasons, choose to put up with it. The Depressive, then, can create utter havoc in a relationship. Refusing to share because they "don't feel like it," they add insult to injury amidst the relational conflict. If only our Depressive would courageously decide to get help by accessing the myriad services available, such as private psychologists or counselors, church counseling programs, or community mental health services!

• *The fierce features of the Rageaholic.* Our final face of destructive silence is the most scary one. The Rageaholic man or woman actually does communicate, at times, but uses words to control, intimidate, and isolate others. Unfair and abusive, he uses his verbal assaults against those less powerful than he. It is a cowardly fight against an unequal opponent.

The Rageaholic uses verbal invasions at times, while at other times he may actually pout or withdraw. Sadly, his periods of rage may be the only times when he feels any sense of control over his world. He is threatened by all of his feelings, except anger. That feeling he knows well, and uses it skillfully.

As with the primitive infant in a tyrannical temper outburst, the Rageaholic does get others to respond. Perhaps he wouldn't need to use such violence if he'd developed other skills for gaining a listening ear. The infant is excused for not having gathered a repertoire of tools for effective communication; the man (or woman), though, is without excuse. It's time to give up such infantile maneuvers. Time to grow up and relate to others with the skills that are accessible to us all, if we'll only exert a little effort.

Enjoy the Goodness of Soulful Silence

I hope I haven't given the impression that all silence in a relationship is destructive, manipulative, or hurtful. In fact, there is a silence that is filled and filling, without destructive effects. Not every silence is a detractor from marital communication. All of us need time and space to recharge our batteries, and couples can give this gift to one another.

In our society, it's often considered a waste of time to sit and reflect. We're encouraged to manage our time, to be productive, to be engaged in purposeful activity. However, we would do well sometimes to leave our agendas behind and indulge in a silence that places no demands on our attention. This might be a time of deep breathing and quietness. A time of going fishing and watching the sun's reflections on the water. A time of soul-searching at the altar of God. A time of "soulful silence" can be just what two people need to rejuvenate their life together, including their sexual relationship. Solitude and silence can restore the soul and psyche. It can be used for the pursuit of peace, not persecution.

The Exhilaration of Being Understood

Remember when you first fell in love with your mate? Ahh, the heady world of new-found romance! It was a safe place where we were accepted for who we are and what we think. In the springtime of love we were gazed at lovingly, perhaps even cooed at on a slightly more adult level.

How intoxicating! Why? *Because another is listening intently and seeking to understand us.* To be understood is a profound and wonderful experience, one that needs to be duplicated again and again in a loving relationship.

Understanding your spouse takes a significant effort, however. Just as in the early stages of your relationship, you gave your partner undivided attention, later, as the distractions of life encroached upon your time, you probably put less of your attention into active listening. Yet the *intention* to give undivided *attention* is the hallmark of mature communication. It is the means of understanding and being understood—with the ultimate goal of becoming "real" with one another.

The Means: Communicating Maturely

It may seem that *mature communication* remains out of reach for the average person. I fear that I have made us all sound like barbarians. In some ways that may be true. We are a society lacking civility. To me, what is most apparent is our childish nature. We seem to be fixated at a very early stage of development where we simply demand that our needs be met. If they are not met, we resort to some vengeful form of blackmail, reminiscent of the "terrible twos." While I do not want to shame us for

Strategy Steps
Rage or Restraint?

Venters need to exert more control, to think before they speak and shriek. This is absolutely crucial: introducing a moment of reflection, thought, consideration before dishing it out. It is, in fact, this interlude between an angry impulse and the urge to act on it that affords venters the possibility of not hurling anger like a weapon at one another. Delay a response until wrath ebbs and you have the space inside yourself to find words to express your hurt rather than launch an attack. Thoughtful silence is a venter's most powerful agent of change.

Venters need to replace their angry abandon with restraint. To achieve this, you can consider these new options:

I don't have to act on my impulse.

I don't have to say what's on my mind at the moment.

I don't have to be rude.

I don't have to keep on fighting.

I don't have to answer an accusation.

I don't have to bring up the past.

I don't have to raise my voice.

I don't have to threaten.

I don't have to respond in kind.[2]

Strategy Steps

Insert Yourself into the Facts

Here's an exercise to help you steer your spouse into sharing noncombative opinions and to eventually break your relationship out of a vicious "fact cycle."

Consider this conversation as an example:

"What are you watching on TV?"

"The playoff game."

"Who's winning?"

"The Yankees."

"What are you doing after the game?"

"I'm going to bed. I have to work early in the morning."

This couple is not communicating in any real way. Now watch: by adding just one sentence to each question, this wife could get him going in a deeper direction.

"What are you watching on TV? I'll watch with you."

"The playoff game."

"Which team are you rooting for?"

"I like the Rangers, but the Yankees are winning."

"Uh-oh. What inning is it? Is there any way the Rangers can come back?"

"The bottom of the sixth. Yeah, they have a fighting chance."

"Well, after the game we'll go get some ice cream before you go to bed, and you can tell me about your day at work."

He may repeat his desire to stay with the game. But at least you tried to get him to go deeper. Don't ever apologize for it.[3]

these traits, I want to challenge us all to grow up. With that in mind, here are four steps any couple can take to deepen their level of communication:

First, you must agree, no matter what, that you will regularly communicate with one another. In the initial stages of a relationship this is easy. There's so much to learn with each other, and there seems to be so little time. But as time goes by, the complications of adjustment create difficulties. A routine settles in as we make our way through finding a job, raising a family, and settling our own personal issues. So make the commitment, right now, that you will work hard to keep those lines of communication open to one another. Most important, commit to talk even when you are moody and want to back away into silence. (This can be the ultimate weapon in a relationship!)

Second, you must steadfastly avoid denial. Can you agree that things need to be improved right now? If left unchanged, the relationship will continue to deteriorate. Believing that there is no problem, or that things will heal themselves, is called denial. Deny it in your relationship!

Third, you must commit to regular reality checks. Relationships need regular attention. A withering relationship left alone will surely die. So, practice checking in with each other and asking how each partner feels about the relationship. Take a regular evening out with one another, dedicated to learning how both of you are doing. A date works wonders. You might also schedule an annual weekend retreat to evaluate the past year and develop goals for the year ahead. Whatever you plan, remember that the best thing you can give to your children is happy parents!

Fourth, you must develop, in advance, a standard way of handling the "heavy" emotions whenever they arise. In other words, you will agree on a set plan that will take over automatically whenever one of you expresses hurt, frustration, or anger. Maybe it's a simple rule that says you will only use "I" statements while taking turns speaking and listening—no accusations allowed. Or maybe you'll choose a plan that flips you both into comfort-giving for the first half hour, rather than letting either spouse attempt problem-solving. For example:

Linda, arriving home: "Boy, I'm really ticked off at my boss right now! He yelled at me again!"

Dick's typical response—getting angry, and spouting "solutions" to her problem: "Why don't you just go over to the Personnel Department and complain? I wouldn't take that. You should be more assertive! Don't let him get away with it. The conversation escalates until both are hurling accusations at one another. It's ironic, because Dick loves Linda and just wants to help her.

Possible alternative: Immediately, both partners recognize it's time to put "our comfort-plan" into action—

Dick: "Let me hold you for a while right now, like we agreed. Later, I'd like to just listen to your problems without trying to solve them . . ."

OR:

Dick: "I can see you're pretty angry. We agreed we'd take some 'time out' at times like this. So I'll check back in with you about this later tonight, okay? I do care."

Obviously, anger is a primary communication roadblock. Physically and emotionally, anger narrows our vision and closes our hearts. Angry, we are prone to blame, catastrophize, and generally distort things. Practice recognizing your emotions, check your self-statements, and have a plan that you will both become accustomed to. That way, you won't end up attacking each other—something neither of you really wants to do.

Good, mature communication will be like money in the bank when it comes to saving your marriage. There are several tips to keep in mind along these lines. Each of these DOs and DON'Ts is important for keeping the lines of communication open:

DO *make "listening" into an action word.* Here you give your partner your undivided attention. This includes maintaining eye contact, using an open body posture that faces your spouse, and making comments that encourage fuller sharing. This type of listening avoids asking questions that are just rhetorical accusations or that can be answered with a mere "yes" or "no." Instead, use questions that deepen understanding. Examples:

Dick: "When I was a kid, Dad told me I could just learn about sex at the library."
Linda: "Are you kidding? Why did he do that?"

A better alternative: "How did you feel about that? How do you think that has affected you?"

Dick: "I'm so bored at work that I can hardly stand it!"
Linda: "Hey, weren't you the one who chose this job?"

A better alternative: "How have you thought about dealing with it?"

Dick: "I just lost the Smith account today."
Linda: "Couldn't you have finessed that guy a little more?"

A better alternative: "That's gotta be a bummer. What level of hurt are you at right now?"

DO exercise active empathy. With active empathy you repeat what the other person is saying, in your own words, to convey that you are with him emotionally. You reflect back to him what you hear him saying. This technique requires the self-control not to be preparing your rebuttal while your spouse is talking. Really listen to him! And notice how good it feels when he practices in-depth listening to you. Examples:

Jane: "I feel like I'm just getting older—and it really shows."

Rob: "No you're not! C'mon, snap out of your rotten mood!"

A better, reflective response from Rob: "That must be discouraging, Honey. You're feeling a sense of loss right now, is that it?"

Jane: "You never just hold me anymore!"

Rob: "That's not true! I know I held you last week."

A better, reflective response from Rob (extending a hand): "Feeling a need for closeness?"

Danger Here!

Steer Clear of Unhelpful Questions

Avoid "shut down" questions when talking with your spouse. Aim for open-ended comments that make him or her want to share more. Likewise, steer clear of interrogative questions where she might feel she is being grilled or pumped. We sound like detectives when our questions . . .

• Demand an answer:

"Let's get to the bottom of this, okay?"

"Can't you see I need to know this now?"

• Are harsh in tone:

"Aren't you tired of keeping this in?"

"You ready to 'fess up yet?"

• Smack of accusation:

"You could get help if you wanted to, right?"

"Are you using your problem to keep a distance between us?"

• Sound unsympathetic:

"Doesn't everyone have problems?"

"Remember when I went through the same thing?"

• Are interrogative:

"Why didn't you move out?"

"Why didn't you complain?"

Jane: "Mom could've told me exactly what to do!"

Rob: "When are you going to quit longing for the old days? Isn't it time to grow up a little?"

A better, reflective response from Rob: "You're missing your mom these days, huh?"

DON'T fail to ask for clarification while checking for perceptions. Similar to asking questions, here you ask for clarification about what the other person is talking about. You may want to tell him that you are hearing such and such, but you are really wondering if that is what he is saying. Your spouse will appreciate your efforts to accurately hear him. With perception-checking you ask whether what you are hearing is accurate. So often, what you thought you heard is not what someone is trying to convey. Keep asking until you get it right! Examples:

"Let me see if I understand. Are you saying that . . . (repeat what you have heard)?"

"I'm not sure I'm really hearing you. Just to be sure, could you run that by me again?"

"Here's what I think you're saying . . . Is that about right?"

"My idea is this . . . . But is that what you're thinking too?"

DON'T belittle a perception—or the right to have it. Many of us hold on to our point of view with an ironclad certainty. We tend to see our point of view as the only right one, rather than recognizing that other perspectives are possible. Of course, the tighter we hold on to our position, the greater the conflict. While it's difficult, it is important that each spouse has the right to his or her own perspective. Therefore, couples shouldn't be working to change their partner's opinions when they have a disagreement.

Yet restraint may be harder than you think.

Perhaps even harder than acknowledging our spouses' points of view, and their right to have them, is developing the ability to understand their point of view. It may seem impossible at times, but I assure you that if you will open your heart and loosen your grip on your own perspective, there is room for two differing opinions on the same topic.

The Goal: Becoming "Real"

Practicing these tested communication tools, which we know to be helpful, will assist you in transforming the way you talk to your partner. You will notice the emotional climate warming up. You'll move from silence into sharing, into deeper intimacy. In other words, you'll become more real with one another.

Several years ago I participated in a two-year program for spiritual direction, a special listening art familiar to Catholics and Episcopalians (among other groups). It was both a profound and stretching experience for me. In the process I practiced learning to listen for the movement of God in my life while helping others do the same. This involves listening with the heart as well as with the mind. One writer on this topic has said that the spiritual director is one who aspires to be a facilitator as well as an awakener of what is already there. It is one who takes seriously the Hebrew meaning of Jesus' name—*Yeshuah*—"opening up, liberating, making space, setting free, taking away confinement and limitation."[5]

Strategy Steps
Finding Middle Ground

Have you mastered the skill of compromise? It's a strategy that will save you hundreds of arguments while depositing much goodwill into your marital love bank. The first step is to change the tone of the argument. Here are some examples of statements that can do it, while moving you both toward the place of "agreeing to disagree":

"I can see why you'd feel that way. And I'd like to try that point of view on for size. As I understand it . . ."

"I suppose I could be wrong about this. If I were to look at it from your perspective, tell me how you'd . . . "

"Hey, maybe in a way we're both partly right. For example . . ."

"Just for a moment, suppose I came around to your way of thinking. Tell me more . . . "

"I want to be sure to understand your position. Because I know there's going to be a way to compromise here. . . "

"Just as an experiment, consider it from my perspective for the next three minutes. . . "

I have often thought that this model of listening is appropriate for marriage, as well. What if we could be our spouse's best spiritual friend? What if we listened to one another with our hearts, and simply called forth in our partner what was already there? What if we assisted him or her in being set free from emotional and spiritual entanglements? It would involve us in listening for our partner's life themes and deep passions, sensing the feelings and motivations that exist far below the surface. Perhaps, like the children's story of the *Velveteen Rabbit*— where a beloved toy was so loved that it eventually came to life—our "story" with one another could be thoroughly life-giving, as well. For when we are loved enough we too become more "real." After all, love is the one thing that frees us to be all that we were meant to be.

> Dear friends, now we are children of God,
>   and what we will be has not yet been made known.
> But we know that when he appears,
>   we shall be like him, for we shall see him as he is.
> — 1 John 3:2

See Dick and Jane Grow Up

There is so much power in our words, the power to hurt or to heal. Both Dick and Jane have often used their words to hurt, though they knew, as do we, that it damaged their relationships. God did not create them to tear one another down, but to build up and honor one another. Suppose they began to do that?

Imagine a Heart-Change in Dick . . .

Dick was frustrated and decided to be direct in his questions. "Linda, tell me the truth. If you're not having an affair, what's wrong? Did something happen to you when you were a kid? Did someone molest you or something?"

In an unusually candid moment, Linda said, "Yes, if you have to know. My uncle molested me from the time I was eight until I was eleven. I told my parents about it but they never did a thing to him. I hate them for that."

"Oh, great!" Dick said. "So I can thank them for the mess we're in. So, can you see how it's wrecking our lives now?"

"No, I don't think that has anything to do with what's happening between us," she replied. "I told you. You're too pushy and just want it more often than I do. The more you push, the more I back away. If you'd give me some space it would happen more."

"Well, now I understand why you keep saying that . . ."

"I don't know," she answered quietly. "I don't like to talk about it or think about it. I feel better if I just pretend like it didn't happen."

"But it did happen. And you're still carrying around all this hurt about it. But what can I do to help?"

"I don't know, Dick. I just don't know."

For the moment Dick and Linda felt closer to one another. Many of their words hadn't been particularly kind. But they were at least honest and direct. They were actually talking about a very sensitive issue, though far from solving the problem. Linda's trauma still haunted her and could be ignited by any number of "triggers." When the flashbacks surfaced, it wreaked havoc with her emotions. A heart change for Dick was going to require great courage and patience. He seemed to be attempting the first small steps.

Imagine a Heart-Change in Jane . . .

In the car, Rob tried to discuss the sermon but noticed that Jane was unusually quiet.

Strategy Steps
Getting to the Heart of Things

At what level are you most often communicating with your spouse? Consider these four typical levels, and remember: It's possible to go deeper!

Level 1: Engage in Small Talk. These are tidbits of talk like, "Got a letter from Mom today" or "Kerry has a doctor appointment at two." Relationships need a lot of this kind of conversation, but there's much more to communication than small talk!

Level 2: Explore New Ideas. Ideas can be liked or disliked, embraced or dismissed. If we attach any of ourselves to our ideas, sharing them is a little like stepping out on an icy pond. But great things can happen when couples explore their ideas.

Level 3: Share Your Opinions. Opinions carry emotions, bits of ourselves, our beliefs, values, and convictions. Good relationships value the free expression of opinions. Learn to seek out each other's opinions.

Level 4: Move on to Emotional Sharing. This kind of sharing carries our hearts. It makes us "feel" like we're in love. We're sharing at this level when we think, "It's like he knows me!" or "We just connected!" or "We stayed up and talked 'till three in the morning!"[6]

His efforts to make conversation fell flat; something was definitely wrong.

"What's up?" he questioned. "You're quiet. You seem to be a million miles away."

She looked at Rob, who had taken one hand off the wheel and gently placed it on her leg. She appreciated his touch but was struggling with what to say. Part of her wanted his support, and part of her wanted distance.

"You know, Rob," she replied cautiously. "I'm not sure what to say. I'm struggling with some issues but I'm not quite ready to share them with you yet. Can we talk about it a little later today?"

Jane became lost in her thoughts once again, remembering how it was so long ago. . . . While her family had enjoyed the many privileges that accompanied her father's military rank, there was also an absence of demonstrable warmth and affection. Jane was left wondering about how much she was really loved. There was an emotional chill in her parents home not overcome by the furnace.

To compensate for the endless hours of work her father had to spend in his important position, Jane was often taken to the city with her mother to—guess what?—shop. Her mother seemed to use shopping as a way to make up for the emotional warmth that was missing at home. Jane remembers many days when she and her mother would shop for clothes for the next military gathering where they were obligated to "look good." While there was some enjoyment to it all, after awhile it failed to help in soothing the rejection she felt from her father and even, to a lesser extent, her mother.

"Look," said Rob. "I know there are things that you are working on, and I want you to know I'm happy to listen. No miracle cures, but I have two good ears."

Jane looked at Rob and smiled. She placed her hand on his as they headed home in a peaceful silence.

Think and Discuss

1. What stage would you say that your marital relationship is in today: Ideal, Ordeal, or wanting a New Deal?

2. What have you done to contribute to the strengths, and weaknesses, of the relationship?

3. Which face of silence do you most often wear? How did you develop that style?

4. What first step could you take in transforming your silence barrier into a communication bridge?

Implementing Your "Marriage Makeover" Plan

Note: Each spouse should take time, in advance, to jot his or her responses to these questions on a separate sheet of paper before coming together for sharing and discussion.

"Growing Up" Step #5:
Moving from Silence to Sharing

Key task: *Confront the unhealthy silence within you, while learning and practicing good communication skills.*

1. Together, review the vignettes at the top of this chapter. Respond, and discuss:

• *Linda comes to you, her best friend, and asks: "How can I respond the next time Dick starts bemoaning the state of our sex life?" How would you counsel her?*

• *You are Rob's best friend. He says to you: "Every time Jane and I start to have a significant conversation, things break down. She usually clams up, so what am I supposed to do?" What would you tell Rob?*

2. If I had to choose one of the "silent faces" that most closely resembles my own, I'd have to pick:

___ the Pouter

___ the Onerous Introvert

___ the Depressive

___ the Rageaholic

• *Discuss the effects on the marriage of wearing your particular "face." Then talk about your conversational tendencies with your spouse. Seek a deeper level of understanding here!*

3. When have I found silence to be especially meaningful and healing in my life? In my marriage?

4. Do we "communicate maturely" in this marriage?

___ *Yes! Here's how I know:*

___ *No! Here's how I know:*

• *Together, make a list of three changes you'd both like to make in your communication patterns:*

(1) _____.
(2) _____.
(3) _____.

5. Review the DOs and DON'Ts for keeping the lines of communication open. Then discuss:

• *How could we each make listening more of an action word?*

• *Here's an example of empathetic listening that each of us could try to put into practice:*

• *How well do we check our perceptions during a serious conversation?*

• *Do we have any problems with belittling our mate's perceptions or opinions? How can we improve in this area?*

6. Take a moment right now to ask your partner what it would take to improve your relationship. Be prepared for some honest feedback. If you will listen closely to the feedback, and act upon it, your relationship will undoubtedly improve!

6 Saying "I'm Sorry"

O uch!" said Jane. "You hurt me!"
"It's not my fault," said Dick.
"Yes!" said Jane. "See my hurt!"

Dick and Linda were fighting again. It was a screaming, yelling, hollering match. "I make one simple comment about our sex life, and you blow up," Dick said. "You know I'm right about this. You get upset about something I've done, and there goes our love life for the next month."

Their relationship had been unsettled for some time and had affected their intimacy. But when Dick decided to make a sarcastic comment about her unavailability to him, she decided she'd had enough.

"Oh, one simple comment," Linda said sarcastically. "Just one more nice comment from Mr. Sensitivity! You know just the thing to make me warm up to you, don't you? Just treat me like I don't matter, and that will sure win me over."

* * * * * *

"Jane," the nurse announced. "Won't you please come in?"

The nurse was friendly enough, but that didn't allay her anxiety about the appointment. She'd been having stomachaches for several months now, and she feared the worse.

"Please step into this room and put on the robe," the nurse said. "I'll be right back to take your blood pressure."

Jane's blood pressure was fine, but tests confirmed the possibility of an ulcer. She would be placed on medication as a preventative measure to try to ward it off. She was encouraged to seek counseling, as well, to deal with the stress she carried around in her stomach.

As Jane left the office, she became angry again. She hated the fact that she now had to take medications for . . . for her *emotions!* Yes, she was under stress, but who wasn't?

And she hated Rob confronting her more lately.

She decided that she wouldn't tell him about the findings. It would feel too much like an admission of some kind of guilt.

Hard to Admit Being Wrong?

Why is it so hard to say, "I was wrong"?

While it may sound like a simplistic explanation, I believe much of the problem lies in us feeling *hurt* and *wronged*. As children we demand a fair world, which, of course, we all know does not exist. Yet, little rankles children more than when they feel they're being mistreated. It doesn't matter to them that their view of the world is distorted. If they feel they're getting a "raw deal," they aren't likely to act generously by apologizing.

But even as adults—when we feel hurt and wronged—underneath our cool exteriors we long to get our fair share, and we manipulate to get it. And it's going to happen over and over, because an *un*distorted view of the world shows that we live in a society generally ruled by:

Scarcity versus plenty;

Me versus you;

Competition versus cooperation;

Consumerism versus simplicity;

Taking versus giving;

Fear versus trust.

Consider this list for a moment. If you agree that these principles rule the day, it's indeed a sad commentary on our society. Reality bites. It hurts and stings when we are passed over for a deserved raise. It hurts when a trusted friend forgets a noted accomplishment. It hurts when our spouse is unfaithful. It hurts when a long-time employee steals from us. People that we trust can be insensitive and hurtful, and the natural inclination is to seek revenge or to recoil in isolation.

It should come as no surprise, then, that "healthy couples" have learned to overcome these slings and arrows of outrageous unfairness. They've learned to deal with the hurts—intentional and inadvertent—that flow from their spouses on a daily basis. In short, they've learned to say "I'm sorry." And they've learned to forgive. If we were to look more closely at the interpersonal dynamics in the lives of such couples, we'd find that a battle is being won against several sets of opposite extremes that continually vie for supremacy in the relationship. Here they are:

Flexibility versus Rigidity

One of the hallmarks of a healthy couple is whether the husband and wife are able to be flexible in their ways of doing things. Unfortunately, we grow accustomed to doing things a certain way, even though it may be a highly dysfunctional way. But when it's time to change, the healthy couple is able to reevaluate and shift gears. On the other hand, the unhealthy couple will cling tenaciously to their old ways, even though it may be killing them.

I'm reminded of the fact that when NASA launches a shuttle it actually flies off-course about 90 percent of the time; Houston spends the majority of its time making small corrections. The same is true of a championship football or basketball team. The huddles are filled with the clamor of barked orders that attempt to make corrections to a pre-designed game plan. *Flexibility is the key to any successful team*—including the success of a couple in marriage.

Open or Closed versus Balanced

Yet another dimension that is critical in a marital relationship concerns being open or closed. This is closely related to the issue of being flexible, but is slightly different. When a couple is "open" they are available to new information and then adjust accordingly. This is good!

However, there is a danger of being too open, letting others influence them inappropriately and unnecessarily. Unhealthy openness is illustrated by the wife who had to consult her mother every time she fought with her husband. Not only did she consult her mother, but she brought several friends into the conflict, as well. They gathered to discuss how wrong her husband was and to

Self-Check

How Flexible Are You?

What do you do when change is suddenly demanded? Choose the response below that comes closest to the way you have typically handled the need to adjust in the past:

• *Scenario: My husband comes home and announces: "Let's find a realtor! I've just decided to accept a job out on the West Coast. Man, this is going to be great! How soon can we start packing?"*

____ I burst into tears, throw a plate into the fireplace, and begin setting the kitchen curtains on fire.

____ I say: "What? I just got through decorating this house the way I wanted it— and this is what you do to me? No way! Don't forget to write once in a while."

____ I say: "Wow! This is certainly sudden! Can we talk all about it? Because I'm definitely wanting to explore how I'm going to adjust. If it's really the right thing to do, you know I'll give it the ole college try. And I know you're going to hear me out too."

My actual response to a similar situation in the past (talk about it with your spouse):

_____

_____

_____

• *Scenario: My wife walks in and says: "I know this hairstyle is a little different, but I told the stylist to give me something more 'contemporary.' I like it, though I didn't think it would be so crew-cut like on the left side. Honey, what do you think?"*

____ I take one look and walk out of the room, slamming the door behind me.

____ I say: "It would be nice to have a wife who knows how to look just a little bit feminine once in a while. Why do I feel like I'm married to a pro wrestler?"

___ I say: "Whoa! I can see that you're enjoying experimenting with your 'look.' I just love your spirit of adventure." Followed by a hug and kiss.

My actual response to a similar situation in the past (talk about it with your spouse):

_____

_____

_____

• *My spouse's parents arrive from out of state, walk into the living room and say: "We'd like to stay for about three weeks. You see, our contractor needs that long to finish the remodeling. . . . Say, what's for dinner tonight?"*

___ I jot a note on the wall in crayon that says: "See you in three weeks, Babe."

___ I immediately pull my spouse into the kitchen and whisper: "Well, well, well. Once again our lives are sabotaged by your parents! Okay, but just don't expect me to lift a finger to make this coming little train wreck any easier to deal with!"

___ I say: "This is a real surprise! Suppose we all talk this over for a while, because I'm sure everybody's routines will be affected. We can talk about the finances, possible hotel rental, meals, transportation, the kids, household chores, and all the other issues. This should be a challenging exercise in problem-solving for all of us—but together we can do it!"

My actual response to a similar situation in the past (talk about it with your spouse):

_____

_____

_____

confirm just how right she was. These friends and family took up the battle against her husband and inadvertently assisted in creating great pain in the marriage. This kind of openness is not helpful.

A closed relational system keeps secrets and lives by the principle that "our relationship is nobody else's business." This is good, to a point. But if this couple keeps up the façade that "all is well" in the home (when it really isn't) and pretends that they need no accountability or input from others, then the relationship will stagnate into dysfunction.

So, if we don't want a totally open system, and a completely closed system doesn't work, what are we looking for? The answer is that we need a balance between these two, just as we are looking for a balance between flexibility and rigidity. The perfectly healthy couple lives with flexible rules and adjusts as their circumstances change. They are open to feedback from others, but they don't talk to just anyone about their conflicts. They listen to counsel but make decisions together, based on their careful, prayerful consideration of the input. In other words, they strive to be flexible, but consistent within that flexibility. They're open to new ideas, but choose new input carefully. They have solid boundaries, but the boundaries aren't impermeable.

It's a careful and delicate balance. Perhaps that is a good way of describing marriage!

Arrogance versus Vulnerability

Here's where the "See Dick and Jane" phenomenon truly comes into play! When was the last time you had a discussion with a seven-year-old about the benefits of an earlier bedtime? How about a talk with the same child about waiting a few weeks for a longed-for toy? Or how about chatting with this child about the merits of eating just one cookie after dinner? If you've had those kinds of discussions recently you are undoubtedly smiling. Using pure rationality will get you nowhere, fast, with the childish mind.

Arrogance says, "I know everything I need to know. I have thought this through and know that what I'm doing is right for me. I don't need your advice on the matter, thank you." Arrogance, you see, is a form of idolatry, putting the Self on the throne of life. There is little room for others when the Self is enthroned. The needs of this insecure person are so large that they must fill up their world with their own desires, thoughts, and actions. Others' needs are pushed away, leaving them feeling smaller in the presence of such a person.

While arrogance is a normal phase for the growing child, it's hardly becoming to the fully developed adult. It is correctable in the maturing youth but too often intractable in the grown adult.

Self-Check
Is Your Relationship Open or Closed?

Make an "X" on the continuum line to show how open, closed, or balanced your view your relationship regarding the five issues below (you may make a photocopy for one spouse, if you like). Be sure to arrange for a time to discuss marked responses and "specific issues" with your mate!

1. When it comes to receiving advice from one another, we are typically:

_____

| Too Open | Open | Balanced | Closed | Too Closed |

• A specific issue to discuss with my spouse along these lines is:

_____ .

2. When it comes to revealing things to others about our marriage we are typically:

_____

| Too Open | Open | Balanced | Closed | Too Closed |

• A specific issue to discuss with my spouse along these lines is:

_____ .

3. When it comes to keeping secrets and staying private, we are typically:

_____

| Too Open | Open | Balanced | Closed | Too Closed |

• A specific issue to discuss with my spouse along these lines is:

_____ .

4. When it comes to maintaining personal and marital boundaries, we are typically:

_____

| Too Open | Open | Balanced | Closed | Too Closed |

• A specific issue to discuss with my spouse along these lines is:

_____ .

5. When it comes to honestly admitting and facing our true problems, we are typically:

_____

| Too Open | Open | Balanced | Closed | Too Closed |

• A specific issue to discuss with my spouse along these lines is:

_____ .

As you are aware, arrogance, or pride, was instrumental in the fall of humankind. Our human ancestors decided that they could be like God and they made decisions that have affected all of us in perpetuity. Solomon, in his infinite wisdom, has much to say about pride and arrogance:

To fear the LORD is to hate evil; I hate pride and arrogance, evil behavior and perverse speech. —Proverbs 8:13

Pride goes before destruction, a haughty spirit before a fall.—Proverbs 16:18

Better to be lowly in spirit and among the oppressed than to share the plunder with the proud.—Proverbs 16:19

A man's pride brings him low, but a man of lowly spirit gains honor.—Proverbs 29:23

Arrogance is devastating to a marriage. Arrogance says, "I can do no wrong." Protecting the fragile ego, it casts blame on the other person and refuses to admit that it has anything to do with the problems at hand. Because arrogance leads to blame, which creates division, a great chasm can be created in a short time.

David Roberts describes an opposite way of living: "We reach our highest freedom not by asserting our own interests against the world, but by devoting ourselves in fellowship to a way of life that reaches personal fulfillment along with, and partly through, the fulfillment of others. . . . This involves moving forward into a deepened recognition of failure, impotence, and need at many points."[1]

But who of us wants to live in a "deepened recognition of failure, impotence, and need"? My goodness! I certainly don't want to make camp there. How vulnerable I would be! I'd rather rest in a place bounded by self-assurance, competence, autonomy, and strength. Yes, that is where I want to park my carcass. How about you?

Distrust versus Communion

When we're honest, we realize that we bring much of our suffering on ourselves. We do it by expecting so much from one another. When our spouse falls short of our out-of-reach expectations, we begin to lose faith that he or she will ever be able to fully meet our needs. Thus we sow the seeds of distrust within the relationship.

Yet there lies within each heart the longing to be loved and accepted. In fact, we were created for communion with one another, and we spend much of our lives searching for that communion. It's a quality of life for which we were designed by our Creator. Henri Nouwen speaks about this communion, stating that the word "evokes relationship, intimacy, and mutuality, and it makes me aware that the union is not simply the result of personal commitment, hard work, and consistent effort. It is the fruit of friendship, affection and love. . . . There is an intimate connection between this search for communion and the spiritual life as a life in which we listen to the voice calling us the Beloved."[2]

Christ, our Creator, has called us into relationship. Yet, as Nouwen says, "The great tragedy of love is that it always wounds. Why is this so? Simply because human love is imperfect, always tainted by needs and unfulfilled desires."[3] Nouwen goes on to say that the great mystery of forgiveness is that humans

Self-Check
What is the Level of Trust in Your Marriage?

Both of you mark the following statements either True or False (you may make a photocopy for one spouse, if you like). Be sure to arrange for a time to discuss your responses!

T F When my spouse comes home late, I assume it's for a legitimate reason.

T F When I share my deepest feelings, I'm confident I'll be heard and not shamed or ridiculed.

T F I know that our private conversations always stay private.

T F My spouse would never make a large purchase without talking it over with me first.

T F I know my spouse will always "be there for me" when I need support, encouragement, or defending.

T F When my spouse leaves home on a business trip, I never worry about his or her faithfulness.

T F My spouse would never "cut me down" in public.

T F I know my spouse won't subvert my attempts to discipline the kids. We are a "solid front" when it comes to childrearing.

T F Other: (Jot your own statement here):
_____.

T F Other: (Jot your own statement here):
_____.

cannot offer what only God can give. We are stuck trying to exact from others a complete love that can come from God alone.

Pride versus Humility

And so here we are on the doorstep of humility again. Haven't we been here before? Can we talk about change without talking about humility? Probably not.

The very word is instructive for us. Stemming partly from the word *humus*, or soil, we immediately recognize something "grounding" about it. The word suggests lowliness, meekness, that opposite of pride and arrogance of which we have talked.

The Sermon on the Mount describes the qualities of a person who would be blessed. One of the qualities is meekness, having a teachable spirit: "Blessed are the poor in spirit, for theirs is the kingdom of heaven" (Matthew 5:3).

This quality requires that we approach our marriage, and the issue of forgiveness, with the ability to look at the situation from the perspective of what we can learn from it. How is the Lord using your current situation, whatever it may be, to encourage, chasten, or grow you? What is the gift in your situation?

Yes, I will grant you that this perspective is radical. It is not the usual cultural method of reviewing and rehearsing how I am getting a raw deal—and then going to court. There will probably be no line forming outside your door to hear how you are rejoicing in your struggles and what you are learning from them. It is not popular news. But how exciting it is to shift from "poor me" to having an attitude of gratitude!

Humility, then, is a requirement for the healthy marriage. In humility we see that whatever harm has been done to me, I am capable of doing to others. Whatever harm others have done, I also have done in my heart. "There but for the grace of God go I."

Begin with Self-Forgiveness

Everything I've been saying in this chapter hinges on something that may surprise you: *your ability to forgive yourself*. At first glance it would seem that the topic of self-forgiveness wouldn't fit in with the themes of arrogance, immaturity, and childishness. Yet a closer look at the malady of arrogance actually reveals a lack of self-forgiveness in many instances. It seems that we cling to our wounded selves, and this entrapment renders us incapable of forgiving ourselves, as well as others. Let me explain . . .

The Distressing Paradox of Self-Rejection

For many people, the very core of their identity is ensnared in "being wounded." And so, in my professional work I see many that have been wounded. Yet, a paradox has become more pronounced as I've gained insight into some of these dynamics.

The wounded becomes the wounder.

And the wounder has always been wounded.

Suddenly the demarcation lines are not as clear as I once saw them. For example, the research indicates that a large percentage of perpetrators of violence have themselves been physically, sexually, or emotionally violated. In fact, the correlation is so clear that we are able to predict, from an early age, those who will be violent later in life. We simply look at the degree of violence perpetrated upon them in their early life.

Thus, each of us needs the loving hand of self-forgiveness. We must be reconciled to ourselves, beginning to see ourselves not as innocent of wrongdoing, but innocent of the wrongdoing done to us. We can begin to look at the destruction that was caused to our souls and realize that it was not all self-caused. Others have damaged us early in life. We are called to recognize it and forgive—ourselves (for things we've done as a result) and also those who wreaked such havoc in our lives. We are called to take all of this information and to feel its pain deeply, to grieve it fully, and to let its energy spark us toward lasting change. You see, people who have suffered the most in life, are often those whom God most deeply transforms, so that they become the most loving and giving of all people. This is the miracle of grace:

You intended to harm me,
but God intended it for good.
—*Genesis 50:20*

Yet it is this struggle—to take us into self-forgiveness, and move on to other-forgiveness—that stops so many from uttering the words, "I'm sorry." Malcolm France sheds more light on this problem:

If guilt is to be healed, the victim must be reconciled to himself. Were his feelings mainly outgoing, there would be little problem: if he felt nothing but grief at the damage which he had caused to others, reconciliation with them would follow easily. He would have no hesitation in saying "I am sorry." But because his feelings are usually complicated by inner remorse and self-rejection, reconciliation becomes difficult, sometimes even impossible, to achieve. The forgiveness which others would give him is blocked by his inability to forgive himself. Therefore the problem of guilt is nothing other than one facet of the problem of self-hatred.[4]

The importance of an honest appraisal of ourselves is readily apparent. So too is the importance of knowing where to go to rid ourselves of that pesky thing called guilt. Here the Apostle John has some sound advice:

If we claim to be without sin, we deceive ourselves and the truth is not in us. If we confess our sins, He is faithful and just to forgive us our sins and purify us from all unrighteousness. —1 John 1:8-9

The Blessed Prospect of Forgiveness

As I've said, if we want to be happy, as well as live in a reasonably happy marriage, we must be able to forgive ourselves so that we can move on and say "I'm sorry" to others. But suppose our spouse says those wonderful, healing words to us? It's only half of the recipe for marital bliss. In response, we need to be able to offer forgiveness to him or her. Of course, we all know that this is easier said than done. Most of us know that we need to forgive others their human foibles, yet we cling tenaciously to our own wounds.

The story is told of an Irish boxer who was converted and became a preacher. He happened to be in a new town setting up his evangelistic tent when a couple of tough thugs noticed what he was doing. Knowing nothing of his background, they made a few insulting remarks. The Irishman merely turned and looked at them. Pressing his luck, one of the bullies took a swing and struck a glancing blow on one side of the ex-boxer's face. He shook it off and said nothing as he stuck out his jaw. The fellow took another punch at the other cheek. At that point the preacher swiftly took off his coat, rolled up his sleeves, and announced, "The Lord gave me no further instructions." *Whop!*[5]

We applaud this gentleman for his self-control, for many of us would not have waited as long as he did to take decisive action. Yet, did he really demonstrate forgiveness? Maybe yes, maybe no.

For one thing, forgiveness does not mean denying our pain. Many of us are tempted to suppress our pain by giving a quick, obligatory, "Oh, that's okay." To offer genuine forgiveness requires that we acknowledge being injured and let the one who has hurt us bear the responsibility for his or her actions.

Yet forgiveness also does not mean holding another ransom, waiting for another day to recall their misdeed. It means "letting go" of your right to hold their actions against them forever. Most of us are able to "let go" of something temporarily; but letting it go indefinitely, in the face of another insult, is a terribly difficult thing to do.

David Augsburger, who wrote the classic book *Caring Enough to Forgive*, suggests that we not forget that forgiveness is a journey of many steps. Rarely is it accomplished in a single action. He also notes that the heart of forgiveness is not just seeing the other as valuable again, though that is important. He states that forgiveness is "to drop the demands for an ironclad guarantee of future behavior and open the future to choice, to spontaneity, to the freedom to fail again." [6]

If you're like me, you may be feeling a bit discouraged at this point. The idea of forgiving my wife is not always pleasant. I want to hold grudges at times. It's a kind of armor I wear to keep me from being hurt while at the same time allowing some self-righteousness for my flagging ego. I can do a splendid job of playing the wounded warrior. But, alas, it isn't productive in the long run. It doesn't really get me the intimacy I desire, and it's not what God wants from me. It seems, then, that the task is in great measure a spiritual one, and I must rely on the Lord in my life to transform my pettiness into the mature man I want to be. How about you?

> # Partnering Points
> ### Understanding True Forgiveness
>
> Forgiveness is a rather complex thing. Have you thought about it lately? Here are three insightful quotes from author Lewis Smedes, an expert on the nature of forgiveness:
>
> • As we forgive people, we gradually come to see the deeper truth about them, a truth our hate blinds us to, a truth we can see only when we separate them from what they did to us. When we heal our memories we are not playing games, we are not making believe. We see the truth again. For the truth about those who hurt us is that they are weak, needy, and fallible human beings. They were people before they hurt us and they are people after they hurt us.
>
> • Forgiveness: You know it has started when you begin to wish that person well.
>
> • Forgiving is tough. Excusing is easy. What a mistake it is to confuse forgiving with being mush, soft, gutless, and oh, so understanding. Before we forgive, we stiffen our spine and we hold a person accountable. And only then, with tough-minded judgment, can we do the outrageously impossible thing: we can forgive. [7]

See Dick and Jane Grow Up

There is hardly anything more difficult in a marriage than saying "I'm sorry." Offering an apology is so difficult, on the one hand, and yet so power-

Strategy Steps

Moving Into Forgiveness

When we apply the principles of forgiving and being forgiven to any discussion of a couple who wants to "grow up," we see that each spouse will need to take several steps. At the least, they will involve:

• Acknowledging pain and earlier betrayal;

• Talking about fear for the future;

• Discussing options regarding ways to trust one another in the future;

• Understanding and accepting that things will never be perfect;

• Accepting that they may hurt one another again;

• Acknowledging the hurt of not being trusted;

• Sharing frustrations; working with one another to create deeper trust.

fully healing on the other.

As we have been learning in this book, true, lasting change is impossible without God's help. But, with His help we can change, accept our failings, and offer others the gift of a heartfelt apology. Forgiveness, given and received, is one of the miracles we have the honor of experiencing during our short journey on earth. Suppose Dick and Jane were ready to say "I'm sorry"?

Imagine a Heart-Change in Dick . . .

Dick sat speechless as Linda abruptly left the room after their fight. He had said many sharp, sarcastic words that he knew were painful. He had felt hurt by her distance and tried to hurt in return. He was flooded with feelings. On the one hand he felt justified in his biting remarks. It served her right. On the other hand he hated this distance and knew she had a right to recoil.

Linda sat on the couch looking at her bed for the evening. This is certainly not what she wanted. But her heart ached because of the words spoken to her in anger. Was it true? Had she been cold? Had she been punishing Dick with distance?

With only a few feet between them there lay a world of distrust, hurt, and sadness.

Yet both Dick and Linda paused as they envisioned embracing one another and letting their pain ease away. It was that tiny moment that we have all experienced—the great chasm between revenge and reconciliation.

Dick waited for a few minutes and then slipped into the living room. "Can we talk?" he asked tentatively. "I don't want our evening to end this way."

"What you said really hurt, Dick," Linda said. "You can't expect me just to reach out to you after you attack me like you did. You always . . . ." She stopped herself from saying what was in her heart. She knew that an attack on him would just lead to another round of fighting.

"No, I'm not expecting you to warm up to me instantly," he said looking at her. He walked over to the couch and sat down. "We don't even have to talk about the issue again. I just want to stop hurting each other. I'm sorry for what I said to you a few minutes ago. I don't want to hurt you."

Imagine a Heart-Change in Jane . . .

Jane sat in her favorite chair after work, fretting about the doctor's findings. More important, she was unsure how to deal more effectively with the stress that was causing her gastrointestinal problems. How would she explain this to Rob?

Sipping on her tea she heard the creaking of the garage door opening. Rob was home. What was she going to say? She decided that it would be better to tell him rather than keep secrets. She'd been secretive in the past, and it had only caused greater problems.

Rob was cheerful as he came into the living room. "What's up? You look comfortable," he said smiling.

"I went to the doctor's today. I have an ulcer," she said. She felt an anger welling up, but decided to move on with her plan to just "report" was happening with her. "Well, not really an ulcer, but some kind of pre-ulcer condition."

"Wow," Rob said astonished. "You've got to be kidding! How is that possible?"

"What kind of question is that?" Jane said with a grin. She chose to see the humor in the question rather than taking it as an accusation. She sensed it would make all the difference in how the conversation would go from here.

"So you don't think it's possible for me to have an ulcer?"

"Wait," Rob said softly. "I didn't mean it that way. I'm not sure what I meant. All I'm saying is that I am surprised. I thought older people who had a lot of stress in their lives got ulcers."

"Yeah," Jane continued. "That's just the point. I guess I am under a lot of stress. But the main thing is, I don't want to take it out on you. I'm sorry that's happened a few times lately. Like when I . . . ."

Strategy Steps

Love Is Saying "I'm Sorry."

Wondering how to apologize in a way that will make a powerful impact? Consider:

Say It Big: If you've had an ongoing argument or if you really put your foot in your mouth, try saying, "I'm sorry" in just as big a way as you blew it. Hang a sign made from a sheet over a freeway overpass, bake a huge, heart-shaped cookie and write "I'm sorry" on it, or fill a room with balloons, each with an apology tied to it.

Say It Face-to-Face: It's wonderful to receive a card or a note, but nothing will strengthen a relationship more than a face-to-face meeting. Catch up with the one you love (wherever he or she is—work, school, home) and walk up to him or her and say, "I'm sorry. I was wrong." Give your loved one a hug and a kiss.

Say It Uniquely: Leave a small gift (perfume, a chocolate treat, jewelry, or tickets for a future date) in a place where your sweetheart will be sure to find it (taped to the car's steering wheel, on the pillow or mirror, or on his or her desk at work). Leave the note with a bouquet of flowers on the front door.

Say It with Sentiment: Write a poem with pen and paper or try magnetic poetry, a set of words that can be arranged into poems on your refrigerator. Quote an apology from your sweetheart's favorite book or movie, or create a gift that captures your humble heart—a song, a painting, or a story.[8]

Think and Discuss

1. In your opinion, are there unresolved trust issues in your marriage? What are they?

2. What have you contributed, both positively and negatively, to get your marriage where it is today?

3. How easy is it for you to admit you've been wrong?

4. Consider the steps of forgiveness. Which are easy for you? Which are more difficult? Why?

Implementing Your "Marriage Makeover" Plan

Note: Each spouse should take time, in advance, to jot his or her responses to these questions on a separate sheet of paper before coming together for sharing and discussion.

"Growing Up" Step #6:
Moving from Grudges to Forgiveness

Key task: *Seek forgiveness—from yourself and your spouse—then offer it liberally.*

1. How easy or difficult is it for you to say: "I was wrong"?

• *Think back through the years of your married life. Make a list of times when you should have said "I'm sorry":*

• *Now take turns apologizing for a few of the things you've listed. (Do much more listening than talking! Seek a new level of understanding and acceptance through this exercise.)*

2. Consider the amount of forgiveness that is given and received in your relationship.

• *Where do I need sincere, heartfelt forgiveness from my spouse?*

• *Where does my spouse desire my genuine offer of forgiveness?*

3. Talk together about how you will forgive and be forgiven in the days ahead. Get specific about ways you could demonstrate your forgiving and "for-given-ness" to one another.

4. Look back at the three scenarios under "How Flexible Are You?" Share your likely response to each one, then discuss: "What one thing could each of us do to become more flexible in this relationship?"

5. Think about the level of trust in your marriage. Complete the sentences below, and then share.

- *I feel that I CAN / CAN'T trust my spouse, because . . .*

- *If trust levels are low, brainstorm together possible solutions to the problem. (IDEA: Try writing a "Trust Contract" that details how you will handle specific trust issues in the future. Sign and date it! Promise to review it on a monthly basis.)*

7 Restoring
the
Adventure

See Dick. See Jane.
"This is no fun!" said Jane.
"Let us have a good time!" said Dick. "What shall we do?
See Dick look and think.
See Jane think too.
"What shall we do?" asked Jane.

Linda sat quietly in the small café, waiting for her friend Karen. It was a nicely detailed, espresso bar where she often came to study.

"Linda," Karen said softly. "Hey, it's good to see you."

"It's good to see you, Karen," Linda replied. "Have a seat."

"You seemed like you were in another world when I walked up. What's happening?"

"It's Dick and me," Linda said. "Sometimes it feels like the only time we connect is when we are talking about the kids. I've been trying to talk to him, but it feels like he doesn't hear me. I'm about to lose my mind."

Karen reached out her hand and touched Linda's hand.

"You two have always been so busy, doing your own thing, I'm not surprised that you feel this way. Actually, I feel that way with Don a lot too. Men can be so self-centered if you ask me."

"What do you guys do about it?"

"Not much," Karen said. "We just kind of learn to live with it and hope that things get better down the road, which they usually do. He has his friends, and I have mine. Sometimes I think that's just the way marriage is after a while. You can't expect the excitement to last forever."

* * * * *

Jane sat at the kitchen table having just eaten a bag of chips with a soda. Tapping her fingers on the table she was unsure of what to do. It was seven in the evening and Rob wasn't going to be home for a few hours. The late fall light was fading fast, and she was feeling restless. It was too early for bed and too late to take in a show. She wasn't sure what was wrong but knew she felt a sense of uneasiness. It was not an unusual feeling.

Jane had been working more hours lately. She invested a lot of time in her work, and things were fine as long as she was busy. It was an exciting, rewarding job. She had a responsible position in the fashion industry as a buyer of women's apparel and could expect to move up the ladder.

But as Jane continued to nurse her soft drink, she wondered about Rob. *Is he really at a business meeting?*

Yet she had no reason to distrust him. They had never had a problem with unfaithfulness. He was a loyal friend, totally committed to their marriage. Why was she feeling this vague emptiness? She tried to shrug it off.

Later that evening, when Rob walked in the door, Jane was aware of checking him out more closely than usual. *Where have you been?* she wondered, although she knew the answer to her question.

She immediately realized that a better question might be: *Where are we going?*

Do You Know the "Weathering" Warning Signs?

Dick and Jane, and Rob and Linda are showing signs of over-busyness and, paradoxically, experiencing the boredom that springs from not connecting regularly. Both of the women desperately want to respark the sense of adventure they knew in the early days of dating and courtship with their husbands. But now, after a few years of work and family routines, they're feeling the effects of marital "weathering"—a special kind of neglect.

I once passed through a town that had not been maintained over the years.

The paint on the road signs had cracked and started to peel. The vibrancy of color on the houses had long since faded into a dull monochrome. Tall, Victorian structures had lost their stately quality. Majestic rooflines sagged beneath the weight of collected debris. Sadly, I could see the decay that had occurred from simple neglect. How many marriages are like those houses?

Actually, every relationship suffers the strains of certain elemental forces, similar to what happens when we leave something precious out in the rain and the cold. In marriage, we contend with many corrosive factors, such as neglecting time together, neglecting our needs for romance, and neglecting the call to adventure. Some of us wake up to reality too late, finding that our marriages have dried up, withered, and faded away.

Plain, drab, dreary—all are symptoms of any marriage that has gone unattended too long. Like a paint-peeled sign, a marriage can weather and disintegrate, as well. The good news is that we can begin to notice the subtle signs of weathering. And we can learn how to make repairs to keep our marriages flourishing and filled with adventure. With those hope-filled premises in mind, let's look at a marriage that's displaying a few warning signs of weathering.

Portrait of a Weather-Beaten Marriage

Shelly was a forty-year-old woman when I met her, though she could easily have passed for fifty. She came to see me at the request of her physician. She would not have come of her own accord, believing that only "mentally ill people" went to see psychologists. (I am forever trying to enlighten people about that false notion!)

She made it perfectly clear that she needed a medical doctor, not a "shrink." Psychologists were, in her mind, not really legitimate anyway. Regardless, her doctor told her that many of her symptoms were psychosomatic—physical symptoms worsened by her stress. She was assured that her physical problems were quite real, but that they were greatly worsened by her emotional functioning.

Over time, along with her increasing physical ailments, Shelly had become a rather "plain" woman. She did not become unattractive overnight, nor alone. She had plenty of help along the way. Her story is a sad one, but it can teach us much.

"I've been married for twenty years," she said, with little emotion in her voice. "My husband, Jess, has been an important part of my life, and I've pretty much lived for him and the kids. I wouldn't have wanted it any other way. Besides, Jess likes me to be around for when he's entertaining other executives. I know that's important for his business. And, well, I don't really mind."

"Have you always been a homemaker?" I asked. "What other things have you done during your life?"

"Oh yes," she said quickly, with a barely noticeable smile emerging. "I was a research assistant at the university for several years. We studied the impact of cholesterol enzymes on the immune system. It was cutting edge work at the time. Well, they've probably solved all of those problems by now."

"Why did you quit?" I questioned. "That must have been hard to give up."

"Jess was moving up at Exxon so fast that even he was surprised at his advancements." Shelly sighed, and paused for a moment before talking again. "He told me we couldn't possibly raise three children, manage a home, and take care of his career all at the same time."

"So how have you and Jess been?" I asked. "I mean, how is your relationship?"

"I really can't complain," she said as she stared at the fountain in my office. "You do what you have to do. You don't have a choice about some things life hands you. You take the good with the bad. Jess has the glamorous side of life, and I keep the home fires burning."

Shelly was becoming a regular philosopher at this point, coming up with numerous rationalizations that I assumed helped her cope with her inner pain. Not wanting to confront her fragile coping mechanisms at this point in our session, I just empathized with her.

"Yes, I suppose you're right. We all have certain obligations, and sometimes we just do them out of loyalty."

Shelly seemed to like my response. "Yes, that's right. It's not the way I would have chosen to live my life, exactly. But it's the way things have turned out."

"Would you tell me a little more about you and Jess?" I continued. "I'd love to hear how you two met, and what you have enjoyed together over the years."

"Well," she said slowly. "Actually, we've known each other since our early college days. We had a great courtship and lots of fun in those days." Shelly smiled at this point. "We really had some good times. That was all before the kids, though."

"What happened after the kids came?" I asked.

"Don't get me wrong," she began. "I mean, they've been the greatest blessing of my life. It's just that I missed out on a few things. But that's over, and I'm just glad for the life I've had. I have some wonderful grandchildren, a full life."

I brought our session to a close as I shared with her the possibility that some of her problems may be the result of a lifestyle that had grown a little dry. This was not easy for her to see.

Shelly was not an easy client, in the sense that she did not want to look very closely at her life. She came for weeks out of obligation to her physician before she began to acknowledge that she might have some things to talk about. Her story, like so many others, was one of hidden grief and pain, buried beneath a façade of polished propriety.

Rage was boiling below the surface with Shelly. Not only had she given up her career dreams and lost her husband to the affections of others (Jess had been involved in several affairs), she had lived a life of quiet suffering out of pride. No one, including the children, knew how desperate things were. Admitting it to herself, though, would start a process of change that would be terrifying, to say the least.

How did Jess and Shelly create such a dull marriage? It takes a lot of work to let a rela-

Technical Talk
A Case of Powerful Learning

In the experimental lab, psychologists placed a dog in a center-divided cage, where the floor would give periodic shocks. The other half of the floor—separated by the wall divider—wasn't electrified. When shocked, the dog came to realize that there was no way out and it would simply have to endure the pain.

However, when the dividing wall was removed, and the dog could seek refuge on the other side of the cage, it did not do so. It had apparently learned to tolerate the pain and would not even experiment with another way to live!

How many of us go through our lives acting as if we can't do anything about our plight, even when several options are close at hand? Few adults know how to identify their painful feelings and deal with the underlying issues that spawned them. Instead, they may demand that their partner be a kind of live-in, pain-killing rescuer. Psychologists have coined a label for this passivity: *learned helplessness*.

tionship get into that kind of shape, just as it takes work to let a beautiful home become weather-worn and pale. Together, Shelly and I began to review the warning signs of weathering in her marriage—

First, Jess and Shelly were constantly doing things separately. As Shelly looked back she could now see clearly that they had habitually chosen for Jess to travel without her while she stayed behind with the children. Rarely would she travel with him, losing precious opportunities to build bridges in their lives. She became even angrier when she remembered that she had asked to go with Jess on more than one occasion, only to have him make excuses for her to stay behind. Now she wanted some answers. Why had he created so many barriers to their being together? What was going on in his mind as they

Partnering Point

Children Come Second!

When I say, "Don't make children the centerpiece of your home" some couples react pretty strongly. They immediately ask: "Well, why not?"

Here's my answer: You don't do it because it gives them the idea that they are the centerpiece of the universe. And if that's true, then where is Almighty God? And where are other people? Doesn't this breed the kind of permissiveness and selfishness that we see in so many homes today?[1]

began to drift apart?

Second, she'd made the children the centerpiece of the family. Her focus on the children undoubtedly created a rift between her and Jess, and may even have been a factor in his choosing to have affairs. You see, the children must be second in priority to the marital relationship. The best thing we can do for our kids is to openly and unreservedly love our spouses. After all, what would be better for any child, in terms of conveying a sense of security and contentment in the home? In a place where love reigns between Mom and Dad, the children are absolutely assured that they too are deeply loved.

Seemingly out of necessity, however, Shelly had grown closer to the children than to Jess. Both had a longing inside for closeness; he had chosen to act on his impulses in an inappropriate way, while she had internalized her pain. Actually, both colluded to bury their pain and the philandering in order to maintain the picture of the "perfect executive and his wife."

Third, they'd ignored the essential role of "time." It takes time to grow a relationship, and Jess and Shelly had precious little of that at critical stages of their marriage. Without time to share their stories and the events that were taking place in their lives, the path between them became overgrown with dried, prickly thistles. No matter what you hear, be assured that among other things needed to grow a relationship, good, quality time is absolutely necessary.

But what is quality time, you ask? Perhaps it's easier to view the opposite: Shelly told of how, when they were together, they had simply watched television or took their children to the movies. Most of their "family activities," it seemed, had been designed to keep them from truly facing one another in give-and-take conversations from the heart. As they grew further apart, it became more difficult to approach true intimacy with one another. Yet they wouldn't speak of their growing distance and the pain it caused. Avoiding emotional discomfort was the easier way to go.

Self-Check

Take a Competitive Quiz

Although some competitive behaviors are hard to spot, others are fairly easy. The following questions will help you pinpoint which competitive behaviors you most frequently use in your marriage. Answer each question with a yes or no.

____ Do you correct your mate in public?

____ Do you often insist on having the last word?

____ Do you usually insist on taking charge of a situation?

____ Do you frequently correct or clarify what your mate has said?

____ Are you often accused of mumbling or talking too softly by your mate?

____ Do you tend to talk on...and on...and on without giving your spouse a chance to talk?

____ Do you find that your mate often needs to ask you for more information when you are telling a story in order that he or she understands what you're talking about?

____ Do you have a habit of beating around the bush when you want something instead of asking for what you want directly?

____ Do you look to your spouse to make most of the decisions because you have difficulty making them?

____ Do you often say, "Do you really want me to?" after your spouse has already said she wants you to?

____ Do you ask your mate what she thinks, and then after she tells you, you explain to her that what she thinks is wrong?

____ Do you introduce subjects for conversation that only you are interested in?

____ Do you frequently change the topic of conversation from what your spouse is talking about to what you want to talk about?

Each question that you have answered with a yes points to the fact that you are competing with your spouse, either to run the show or to be taken care of.

Fourth, they entered the ring at every opportunity. They kept fighting! Like pro boxers, they just couldn't avoid hopping into the ring to (figuratively) duke it out whenever they had a chance. Continual conflict, without respite or "bridges" of joyful communication, is usually one of the primary breakers of relational harmony.

Not all fighting is bad, of course, because sometimes it takes a good fight to clear the air and get the real issues on the table. In other words, it can set the context for genuine communication. But Jess and Shelly seemed to have an unspoken agreement not to talk—or even fight about—the tough issues between them. Therefore they lost the opportunity to do what the Bible commands: "Speak the truth in love."

Fifth, they settled for relational dullness. Jess and Shelly had many problems but buried their heads in the sand and pretended that things were just fine. Not wanting to rock the boat, each found some justification to maintain the status quo. "It's not so bad," they would say to themselves. "We don't have it any worse than others. We're not going to feel those same warm, fuzzy feelings at this age that we felt years ago." And so it went, on and on, until the mountain of denial collapsed under the weight of Shelly's physical symptoms.

The Possibility of Romance-Filled Living

Shelly and Jess had long since let go of the romance in their marriage. What a shame! Romance doesn't have to die over the years. In fact, it can grow more satisfying. That's because the sense of the romantic never really dies in us. We all want to be courted and considered desirable. Without expressing and extending this desire, we age before our time. Instead of life, we experience loss.

It is equally the man's responsibility to initiate romantic involvement. In this case, Jess was a real schmuck for letting himself go physically, potbelly and all, and yet looking outside of his marriage to fulfill his romantic and sexual desires. Rather than using all of the energy he needed to maintain his double life, he could have focused on enhancing his romantic involvement with Shelly.

As their counselor, it was easy for me to see from their marital deterioration that Jess and Shelly's relationship had been dying a slow and painful death. But too often we prepare a marriage for burial when there are still sparks of life within it. Would they be willing to shelter those love-embers while we rebuilt the fireplace of romance?

Time to Restore the Adventure?

It is quite an experience to feel emotionally dead and then gradually awaken to genuine feelings, sights, and sounds. Some of you reading this book may feel that you are, or have been, on the brink of emotional death. Boredom, apathy, and emotional numbing may have been coping mechanisms you used to help you get through the day-by-day vicissitudes of married life.

Regardless of whether your relationship history is filled with physical or emotional abuse, conflict or isolation, you can heal and find new excitement and adventure in your life and marriage. Let's look now at how to repair the damage to a marriage that stems from "weathering" and neglect. It's time to restore the adventure. It really is possible, no matter where you are in your "relationship remodeling" efforts. Here are some of the steps others have found especially helpful—

Step One: Take a Rigorous Inventory

Immediately upon our resolve to make significant changes, we need to sit back and take inventory of our lives. In particular, we need to ask ourselves some questions about how much freedom we feel in our lives. If we do not feel free, our bodies will begin to show signs of premature wear and tear. We will be carrying the strains of unexpressed desires in our bodies, and that will be a burden that becomes quite heavy after a while.

One of the steps of the Alcoholics Anonymous program is "to take a fearless moral inventory" of our lives. The premise is that only after we have looked candidly in the mirror can we see what needs to be changed, and lay out a plan to change it. While it should have happened years ago, it was still not too late for Shelly to honestly assess what was happening in her marriage. Faced with the truth, she then had real choices about what to do with her life. As long as she was living a lie, and Jess was living a lie with her, no significant improvement was possible. In fact, it was a sure, slow path to emotional, and perhaps even physical, death. Denial can kill us!

The opposite of denial is candid reality. "You shall know the truth, and the truth shall set you free." Or, as Daniel Webster said many years ago, "Knowledge, in truth, is the great sun in the firmament. Life and power are scattered with all its beams."

Shelly was not the only person in this relationship who had become deadened to life's potential adventure. Jess himself lived a life "of quiet desperation." You see, he was "programmed" from early on in life to live by several key principles; we call them "Life Scripts" or rules. For Jess, they were:

Work hard;

Be serious;

Get your work done before you play;

Be productive;

Win;

Make a lot of money;

Don't feel;

Don't talk about your feelings;

Be a success.

Obviously, Jess wasn't raised in freedom. You can imagine what kind of background he had—raised by a very successful businessman, a "self-made man" who expected the same from his son. His father just didn't know how to have fun, and he passed that quality on to Jess.

Because of this, it wasn't hard for me to see how Jess could be attracted to Shelly in their earlier years. She was lively, spirited, and sought adventure. These were qualities Jess loved, and they resided somewhere deep within. She gave him hope that one day he too would be able to "let go" and let the child come out to play. That, unfortunately, had not happened. Rather, the overbearing parental figure in him, straight from his father, scolded Shelly for her childish antics. While he tolerated, even enjoyed, her frivolities early on, they soon wore on him, and he stifled her enthusiasm fairly quickly. This atmosphere, then, set the stage for their early marital life.

Seriousness, work, and productivity all ruled their home in the beginning. Rarely would Jess even hint that he wanted a relationship that was meaningful, joyful, and filled with adventure. These were foreign ideas to his consciousness. If there were signs of boredom and fatigue in a relationship, it just meant that a couple was working hard and focusing on the things that really mattered in life—the things listed on Jess's Life Script.

It was all so very practical for him.

His philosophizing regarding the practicalities of marriage eventually wore Shelly down, so that she too began to talk and think this way. Jess's Script became hers, as well. The freedom to be who she was—to think what she genuinely thought, and to feel what she truly felt—was gradually weathered away by the harsh elements in her home environment. The marriage could resist the deterioration only so long. All of these things were issues that Shelly and Jess would need to face, should they choose to take their fearless inventory together.

Step Two: Assume Personal Responsibility

Renewal and restored adventure won't happen if we wait for someone else to walk up to us and offer the perfect love for which we've been waiting. We must actively go out and create it.

Remember that you are Picasso, and the world is your canvas. Be very careful about sinking into a "pity party" where you indulge yourself with feelings of "poor me." Blaming others will not be helpful here. While you are entitled to have your feelings, try not to get stuck in them. They may have some value in guiding you in the direction of what is missing in your life, but then you must take the step of action.

Strategy Steps

How Much Freedom in Your Marriage?

How hemmed in we all are by the "shoulds" and "oughts" of this world! Ready for a change?

Therapist Virginia Satir shared the importance of "The Five Freedoms" in her popular book *Making Contact*. Use them to help you take an honest inventory of your circumstances—which could lead to some exciting new directions.

1. The freedom to see and hear what is here instead of what should be, was, or will be;

2. The freedom to say what one feels and thinks, instead of what one should;

3. The freedom to feel what one feels, instead of what one ought;

4. The freedom to ask for what one wants, instead of always waiting for permission;

5. The freedom to take risks in one's own behalf, instead of choosing to be only "secure" and not rocking the boat.

Shelly took personal responsibility by staying in therapy for over a year. As a result, she can now see things she couldn't see before. She can think for herself rather than merely echo the thoughts of her husband. She can reason out what is best for her, and she finds that freedom exhilarating. She can also feel her authentic feelings without squelching them or transforming them immediately into shame or bodily maladies. And she is learning that emotions are "e-motions," or energy-in-motion. If she would listen to them, she learned, they would be helpful in guiding her to where she needed to be. Her spiritual life has become richer too in the face of her pain. Regular quiet times with God have brought a newfound wisdom.

Here's an example of what I mean: One day Shelly shared that she was sad and afraid. It was a time of uncertainty in her life, and she was frightened because the world she had known for so long was falling apart. (Actually, she was letting walls down so that her old comfortable world would, indeed, slowly disintegrate.) She had more control than she acknowledged, for it was she who was choosing to let the old ways of doing things begin to erode.

The point is, she chose to face her fear and sadness, experience them in all of their depth and pain, and continue forward. You see, there are four primary emotions: Fear, anger, sadness, and joy. We can choose to "have" these emotions and experience them fully—which involves taking personal responsibility for them—or we can choose to try to escape them, push them down, or ameliorate their pain with a "drug of choice," be it substances or codependent relationships. The amazing thing about choosing to stick with our so-called "negative" emotions is that once we plumb the depths of our fear, anger, and sadness, we are released to feel, as well, the fullest depths of our joy. That was the experience of Shelly as she came to the end of her counseling.

"I cannot go back to where I have been," she said. "I've seen something new, something that holds great possibilities for me. I have to see where it can lead me." She paused and looked again at the water trickling down the fountain. She was still afraid, but filled with a sense of joyful anticipation. "I hope God knows what He's doing with me," she said, with a twinkle in her eye.

Step Three: List Exactly What You Want

Now it's time to list what you want from a marriage and state how you are likely to get it. You will need to list not only what you consider the current problems to be, and possible solutions, but also list qualities of healthy married life that you may never have experienced in the past. I suspect that you want things like passion, commitment, faithfulness, loyalty, and integrity. Those are lofty goals, but available to you. You may also want things like fun, excitement, and adventure. These are ingredients for a rich relationship and they too are available to you. But you must include in your action plan exactly how you will create those things in your marriage. Work hard with your partner to get as specific as possible.

While you may not be able to re-create the exact feelings you had on the day you first met, you can develop a deeper, more intimate passion for your spouse. In fact, you must keep the passion fires burning. There is something within all of us that desires the sensual. This includes the sexual aspect of a relationship but is much more than that. It can mean a simple touch, the way you say hello, or how you sit and look at one another while eating. It can include how you dress and how you keep your home. Passion and sensuality will hopefully be a part of your everyday experience.

Step Four: Record Your Action Plan Together

You've heard it before, and it's worth saying again: *If it's not written down, and a commitment made to it, it will not happen.* So, you must commit to four things: (1) keeping a personal journal where you record your feelings, thoughts, and desires; (2) brainstorming with your spouse to develop an action plan, as simple as it may be, describing what you will both do to move toward deeper intimacy (this will likely include sharing from your journals); (3) scheduling regular "check-up" talks to discuss how the plan is going—and to make adjustments, and (4) praying about your plan daily—preferably together. Do we have an agreement?

As you keep your journals and create your action plan, you'll uncover many things that need to be discussed together, things that may have been buried for a long time. And you'll be creating a pattern, or even an obligation, to "speak the truth in love." While it may be very difficult to say it the way it is, to say in a nonthreatening way what is missing in your lives is critical. Things cannot get better until the truth is out in the open.

Step Five: Keep Committing to Romance-Sparking Experiences

Zest and adventure in a relationship spring from a commitment to creativity by both partners. Just as filet mignon every night of the week would become boring, so too relationships can become routine. It takes some energy to change it! So, you'll both need to work at building in experiences that will keep the relationship rich and alive. Let me give you an example.

My wife and I have learned the hard way that we need to have something to look forward to. We make it a habit to do something fun together every week. Some weeks it may be as simple as taking in a show and dinner, or simply roller-blading in the park. We enjoy kayaking on the river, especially during a full moon. On other occasions we will break the bank and book a room at a bed and breakfast at the beach. While those weekends cost a little more, they are a great investment in our marriage and pay wonderful dividends. I highly recommend a commitment to weekly dates and monthly extravaganzas.

Another aspect of creating adventure is treating your spouse as "special," regardless of the circumstances. Men, you can purchase a small bouquet of flowers at the supermarket for about three dollars. Women, a card left on his pillow will make him blush, but he really will appreciate it. These little things are small deposits in the love bank that you will need later when the storm clouds form.

One more thought in this area: You just can't do enough nice things for one another. If you take your spouse for granted he or she will begin to treat you the same way. There is no faster way for the zing to fail than "forgetting" to do those nice little extra things for one another.

Step Six: Live in the Light of Shared Faith

Finally, I must also add the importance of having a shared faith. This truly is a way to knit your hearts together in a common bond. And it will bring a blessed quality of transcendence into your relationship.

You see, there is more to our lives than just what we can see and touch. We were created for purposes much higher than mere self-centered pursuits; our lives are to be filled with giving. Understanding this, and living it out, will allow us to give love when we would rather take love. It will allow us to "see" another's needs and take joy in meeting them. It will also allow us to keep our inner eyes focused on the unseen reward that awaits us after all of our hurts and struggles come to an end.

I heard of a woman who'd been diagnosed with a terminal illness and had been given three months to live. As she was "getting her things in order" she contacted her pastor and had him come to her house to discuss her wishes for the funeral. She told him which songs she wanted, which Scriptures were to be read, and what outfit she wanted to be buried in. She also requested to be buried with her favorite Bible.

"There's one more thing," she said excitedly.

"What's that?" came the pastor's reply.

"This is very important. I want to be buried with a fork in my right hand." The pastor sat looking at the woman, not knowing what to say. "That surprises you, doesn't it?" the woman asked.

"Well, to be honest, I'm puzzled by the request."

The woman explained. "In all my years of attending church socials and potluck dinners I remember that when the dishes of the main course were being cleared someone would usually say, 'Keep your fork.' It was my favorite part because I knew something better was coming, like velvety chocolate cake or deep-dish pie. Something wonderful, and with substance! So, I just want people to see me there in the casket with a fork in my hand, and I want them to wonder, 'What's with the fork?' Then I want you to tell them: 'Keep your fork. The best is yet to come.'"

See Dick and Jane Grow Up

There is something within all of us, created by God, that longs for the eternal. We have desires and are continually pressing onward. We want more.

While these desires have often been perverted, and twisted in a way that only the childish can do, God can transform them into something new and adventuresome. Our marriages can be a journey of two people exploring a wonderful landscape of experiences. We can hold hands and, as Thoreau said, visit a place for the second time and experience it as new. Suppose Dick and Jane attempted it?

Danger Here!
Missing the Almighty?

My pastor does quite a bit of marital counseling. He says that he begins by asking why a couple has sought out his services. After this introduction, he asks whether they have prayed about their dilemma. If they haven't, he questions them as to why they would seek counsel from a fallible human being when the Almighty hasn't even been consulted! In other words, it's pretty dangerous to attempt to run a life—or a marriage—apart from God.

Imagine a Heart-Change in Dick . . .

Dick sat with one of his friends in Starbucks one afternoon after an exhausting bike ride. Both were pleased with the "burn" they'd achieved and felt satisfied with their progressing abilities.

"What a challenging ride!" said Dick. "But I wish Linda would enjoy these things with me."

"What's up with that?" Steve asked. "Why aren't you guys riding together?"

"Well," Dick said. "She has her own things going on and doesn't really like the kind of riding I do anyway."

"Why don't you do the kind of riding she likes to do?" Steve said. "There's no sense splitting up your marriage over a stupid bike. You know, I hardly ever see you guys doing things as a couple. That can't be too good for your relationship."

"As a matter of fact," Dick continued. "I've tried to get her out here riding with us, and she won't come."

Steve laughed and threw his straw at Dick. "Man, you don't even hear yourself do you? I said *why don't you do the kind of riding that she likes to do?* That way, you could be building some good times together."

Dick paused and stared out the window. "I guess I've been doing my own thing for so long that it's a stretch to think about joining her on her outings. Novel idea, I must admit."

Imagine a Heart-Change in Jane . . .

Jane fingered the brochure she'd requested. It was an ad for a bed-and-breakfast lodge on the coast. *Would Rob be interested in going away for the weekend?* Her thoughts raced as she wondered what they would talk about, what they might do, whether they would enjoy their time together.

Jane reflected on the gap that had been growing in their relationship. It had been nearly a year since they had gone away together. It was nobody's fault, per se, but merely an indication of the distance growing between them. She was suddenly sad and a bit nervous. *Does Rob still love me? Does he still find me attractive? Does he notice the growing lines on my face?*

Just then Rob walked into the kitchen. He had a big smile on his face that melted some of her tension.

"What's up?" he said. "You look a little somber."

"Just thinking about us," she said softly. "Do you know how long it's been since we've been away together?"

"Well, is this a quiz?" Rob said laughing. "Tell me you're thinking about whisking me away and treating me to a great prime rib dinner at the beach and I'll follow you anywhere."

"Would you believe a cabin on the peninsula with pizza?"

"It's a done deal as far as I'm concerned," Rob said as he put his arm around her shoulder.

Think and Discuss

1. When considering your love life, how would you rate it on the alphabet from Apathy to Zing?

2. What is one ingredient that is missing, more than others, from your love life?

3. What are some of the patterns in your marriage that you would like to change? How do you envision these changes taking place?

Implementing Your "Marriage Makeover" Plan

Note: Each spouse should take time, in advance, to jot his or her responses to these questions on a separate sheet of paper before coming together for sharing and discussion.

"Growing Up" Step #7:
Moving from Apathy to Adventure

Key task: *Together, walk through the six steps to restoring marital adventure.*

1. Can you relate to the story of Jess and Shelly? Of the five issues in their relationship, which seem most relevant to you and your marriage? Why?

2. Work with your spouse to restore the adventure in your marriage. Set aside some extended periods of time during the coming weeks to go through the six steps laid out in this chapter. You may wish to use these questions and suggestions as your guide:

• *Step One: Take a rigorous inventory.*

Ask yourselves: What things in our relationship have we failed to face, squarely and candidly?

• *Step Two: Assume personal responsibility.*

Decide: What must each of us, as individuals, do in order to contribute positive change to this marriage? (Make specific commitments!)

• *Step Three: List exactly what you want.*

Make lists: Jot down what you want from the marriage. Discuss how you and your spouse can work to get these needs and desires met.

• **Step Four: Record your action plan together.**

Gather: Paper and pencils. Start writing. Get all of your decisions and plans for the future down on paper.

• **Step Five: Keep committing to romance-sparking experiences.**

Plan: Take out a calendar and mark your "dates" for the next three months (Nights out? A three-day weekend? Other ideas?) What creative ideas do you have for sparking romance?

• **Step Six: Live in the light of shared faith.**

Discuss: What role does God play in this relationship? Are we able to pray together about our problems? Can we explore the Scriptures together? What things could we do to enhance our spiritual life as a couple?

8 Enjoying the Marriage

S ee Dick and Jane.
They are married.
They are happy now.
Smile, Dick!
Smile, Jane!

Having surveyed some of the joys and sorrows accompanying the journey to maturity, we've seen how, like Dick and Jane, it's possible for us to retain certain childish traits that subvert our efforts to change. Now, in our adult relationships, these qualities of immaturity cause problems. How often we wish to keep playing in the sandlot in order to escape our nagging adult frustrations! Childhood, even with all its challenges, offered some good places to hide from responsibility.

But we've also learned that it's possible to "grow up" and have a happy, healthy marriage. The principles and techniques I've shared in this book have had that single, heavenly purpose in mind. As we approach the end of our journey together, I'd like to leave you with a few parting words of guidance related to establishing and maintaining the marital joy we so desire. I like to think of them with the concrete imagery of: (1) *tools* for creating a healthy marriage, and (2) *anchors* to keep it stable in rough waters.

Tooling Up for Marital Health

I can't help but wonder at times as to what makes marriage so challenging. Is it our basic differences that scrape against one another? Or does it all boil down to our selfish nature? Whatever the reasons, because of the inherent challenge to unity, we have an obligation to give our best to the relationship. Half measures get us nowhere. We must overcome our inertia and hone some special skills.

Yes, it's hard work. And to do work we need tools. Here are six essential health-creating tools that have helped "fix up" countless marriages:

The Gauge of Goodwill

Nothing will give you a reading of the marital temperature better than checking the level of goodwill that flows—or doesn't flow—between the husband and wife. That's why I ask every couple that comes to counseling to assess their level of goodwill toward one another. What do I mean? Well, I am not asking whether they fight; rather, I'm asking whether they are willing to set some of their differences aside so we can work on the basic issues. If the level of hostility in the room is too high, there will be too many barriers to incorporating new patterns of behavior into their lives. In other words, do they still like each other enough to participate fully in the counseling process?

Extending goodwill is essentially a matter of the heart. No couple can make progress if their hearts aren't in it. Many of us have undertaken a project, but if it is devoid of "heart," it will simply turn into another burdensome chore. So consider where your heart is. While you may have a legal contract that says you're married, the real binding law is that of love. If you do not have a heartfelt desire to please your spouse, all the mechanical moves in the world will disappoint you. The Scripture gives us God's loving assurance, "I will be your God and you will be My people," implying that God constantly holds us in His loving care. What if we had that heart attitude toward our spouse, day in and day out?

The "Money" of Motivation

Yes, money is a tool when it comes to construction projects. Most contractors receive an advance for purchasing a certain amount of materials and labor. It supplies the motivation to get started, to do the job right, and to move forward to completion.

In marriage we need a similar kind of high-energy motivation. For real change to occur we must be motivated to work on issues. If we think of our marriages as a "bank account," then what we have to gain by involving ourselves in the change process must exceed what we will be giving up. Thus we can ask ourselves: *How often have I done the extra unselfish act for my spouse? When have I gone the extra mile for him or her? What did I give that was so meaningful? How long has it been since I said "I love you"?*

> # Partnering Point
>
> A wife is a gift bestowed upon man to reconcile him to the loss of paradise.
>
> —*Johann von Goethe*

On the other hand, we can also consider how often we said or did something that was obviously hurtful, withdrawing marital money from our fragile account. Demonstrate your love through an affectionate actions every day! Create intimacy through small acts of random kindness. These will offset the withdrawals you take routinely from your love account.

Jesus tells us in His parables that a man was so excited about gaining a valuable plot of land that he sold all he had in order to buy it. Our Lord also spoke of a merchant so enamored by a beautiful pearl that he gave up everything else to obtain it (see Matthew 13:45-46). These stories illustrate for us the true cost of obtaining something we find valuable. The question for all of us is, "How valuable is my marriage to me?" Am I willing to "sell all" or be "sold out" for it? Can I sacrifice my self-interest in order to strengthen the marriage bonds of love?

The Stepladder of Schooling

Keep reaching higher! Step up to every opportunity for education about how to make your marriage the best it can be. While goodwill and motivation are the tools to get you started, you'll need to school yourself in the critical issues over the long haul of your relationship.

Far too many of the couples I see in my office want what could be called "a quick fix." That is, they want all the extras and amenities in their envisioned marital dream house without spending any time studying floorplans, costing out materials, and gearing up for some pretty intense labor. They expect happiness to appear and problems to disappear without much effort or understanding on anyone's part. They fail to stay educated about the latest methods for building a lifetime of affection.

I attempt to dispel the quick-fix myth early on. We must all become experts at this thing called marriage. Together, let's keep moving higher on the ladder of learning and understanding.

Self-Check

A Four-Star Pay Scale

Well-managed marriages depend on a kind of reward system, in which they make the payments regularly. Periodically they review the scale and make adjustments accordingly.

Pick yourself as the paymaster and ask what kind of compensation you are handing out. It may help to grade yourself on a four-star scale. How many stars can you circle?

Conversational Pay

Do you provide opportunities for discussion? We watch talk shows and appreciate the conversation of others. But is there plenty of flex time for each partner to verbally express himself? ★★★★

Financial Pay

Each partner needs a designated amount of disposable income to spend on himself without being accountable. Financial liberty is essential to maintaining a free spirit. How do you rate? ★★★★

Dream Pay

There is no better investment than planning a happy future. Looking forward to a cruise of Alaska, a new set of candleholders, a move to another state will do wonders for one's outlook. Do your spirits reach four stars? ★★★★

Physical Pay

Try more touching! We can change our partner, make him or her feel younger, healthier, and more optimistic simply by touching. ★★★★

Opinion Pay

Self-esteem will skyrocket if the person feels someone cares what she thinks. How many stars do you get? ★★★★

Free Time Pay

Each partner deserves a reasonable amount of time to himself. The freedom to pursue individual goals is essential to feelings of accomplishment and self-satisfaction. Where are you here?[1] ★★★★

Technical Talk

Have You Completed Your Stage?

In *Passages of Marriage*, psychologists Minirth, Newman, and Hemfelt offer a developmental analysis of the various "stages" that a marriage goes through over the years.[2] Here's a brief summary of the five passages and some of the key tasks couples must complete if they are to move ahead in healthy relational growth:

Passage 1—Young Love: first 2 years.

Key Tasks/Challenges:

- Two independent persons must become one unit.
- Learn to make responsible choices.
- Build a sexual union.
- Deal with parents' incomplete passages.

Passage 2— Realistic Love: 3rd through the 10th years.

Key Tasks/Challenges:

- Hang on to love after reality strikes.
- Recognize the hidden "contracts" in the relationship.
- Write a new marriage contract.
- Successfully deal with the stresses of childrearing.

Passage 3—Comfortable Love: 11th through the 25th years.

Key Tasks/Challenges:

- Maintain an individual identity along with the marriage identity.
- Say final good-byes to parents.

- Overcome the illusions of perfection: perfect mate, perfect sex, perfect romance, etc.
- Help your adolescent become an individual.

Passage 4—Renewing Love: 26th through the 35th years.

Key Tasks/Challenges:

- Survive imperfection!
- Reestablish intimacy.
- Grieve and accept the losses: youth, parents, kids (empty nest), health, financial dreams.

Passage 5—Transcendent Love: 36th year and on . . .

Key Tasks/Challenges:

- Prepare for retirement.
- Achieve a transcendent perspective— about life and death, loneliness, time, spirituality.
- Accept my one-and-only God-given life.
- Decide what to give the world.

The File of Focus

Day by day, are you shaving away at the distractions? You and your spouse will achieve a nice working relationship by narrowing your focus for deliberate attention to one another. I'm reminded of a friend of mine who's crazy about sailing. He thoroughly enjoys it and can't talk enough about it. When I visit his home, I see countless magazines on the subject and glossy coffee-table books displaying the "beauties" he drools over. And all the framed photos on the walls—he absolutely *loves* sailboats.

He's gotten into sailing, and sailing has gotten into him. In other words, he's focused on sailing and loving every minute of it. Unfortunately, he's in danger of becoming a sailboat widower. If he could only apply half that much love and focus to his marriage!

A file is used to hone and sharpen, scraping away any excess material that would prevent a perfect fit. Take a look around your home, in your working spaces, even in your vehicle. What things there would tell a stranger about the loves of your life? Are these things helping or hindering the bond with your spouse? What about your conversation? Do you mention your mate with loving respect and affection when you speak of your private life? If not, could there be a lack of focus on what ought to matter most—your marriage?

The Pliers of Perseverance

The word *pliers* is plural, because this tool uses two equal parts that must work together in synchronized harmony if they are to be effective. Isn't this a inspiring picture of a good marriage? Any worthwhile accomplishment requires perseverance, and both people must work in unity to achieve it.

Many of us who begin to work on our marriages become discouraged because it is so easy to fall back into familiar routines, keeping certain parts of our lives separate and off limits, pulling back from a full disclosure of our souls. We have deep needs, longings, and hurts. We could bring them to the marriage and be vulnerable with our mates.

We could be hurt!

But more likely we'll receive soul-sharing in return and eventually enjoy a deepened intimacy together. As we keep cutting through our trials and tribulations together we grow stronger and more confident as a couple. In short, we become thoroughly happy to be in this relationship! All of this can happen, with God's help. Thus the Apostle Paul challenges us to press on, "being strengthened with all power according to his glorious might so that you may have great endurance and patience" (Colossians 1:11).

The Hammer of Humility

No, don't use it to "hammer" your spouse! But let your humble approach generate in you a deeper commitment and a more loving submission.

Submit to one another out of reverence for Christ.
—*Ephesians 5:21*

We have already discussed this topic at length, pointing out that it is not through our personal strength that we will accomplish great things. We need to be humble colaborers with Christ to accomplish the work He has for us in our marriages. When we're tempted to crawl into a hole and feel sorry for ourselves, it's best to remind ourselves of our frail humanity. That is not to say we can rest on our laurels, but rather we must be keenly aware of our vulnerability.

These tools, then, are a part of what we need in order to build a home where love can flourish. But a marriage is more like a houseboat than a countryside estate! What will keep us steady and stable when the winds of crisis whip up some threatening waves?

Anchoring for Stability

Consider with me the role of an anchor. In virtually all boats of any size, an anchor keeps the ship grounded, positioned right where it should be. Today many of us are attempting to float a marriage without an anchor. While we can get along for a while without one, sooner or later we begin drifting from the safe shores of the dreams and promises of our wedding day.

Yet we need anchors more now than ever before. We are working longer hours, getting less sleep, eating poorer diets, and, in ever greater numbers, jumping into the stream that twists and turns toward divorce court (in my town the divorce rate hovers at 70 percent). We need anchors that can withstand every subtle current pulling us toward troubled waters.

Are You Weighing Anchor with These Tasks?

Author and marriage expert Judith Wallerstein lays out nine tasks that tend to preserve marriages. I'd like survey these with you, offering my own comments along the way.[3] She speaks of "tasks" but, in my mind, their actual function is to serve as "anchoring influences" in marriages over the years—if we do, indeed, make use of them. As we proceed through these anchoring tasks, consider which ones are evident or missing in your own marriage.

1. Separating from the family of origin. Wallerstein suggests that the first task of any healthy marriage is to separate psychologically from the family of origin and simultaneously create a new kind of connectedness with the parent's generation. We need not move a thousand miles away to accomplish this task. Rather, it is a matter of following the scriptural mandate: at the right time we leave Mother and Father and cleave to our spouse.

You may be surprised at how often this is a problem in marriages. Kendra and Douglas had been married a scant twenty months when he began to see the writing on the wall. Whenever Kendra was upset or quarrelling with Douglas, she would head downstate to spend time with her parents. Douglas grew to resent her departures and his in-laws. As she told the story, however, she needed support from somewhere and felt she wasn't getting it from Douglas. And her parents weren't inclined to send her away from the door. Thus the marriage "boat" became weighted down with excess baggage—two other persons (Mom and Dad) figuratively shared the vessel with them. Would they all capsize?

Douglas obviously felt threatened. Not only did Kendra not stay to work through problems with him, but he also imagined her parents standing against him without hearing both sides of the story. Douglas came to resent the intrusion of her family into his life. He wanted his wife back emotionally, spiritually, and physically.

Upon the counsel of their pastor, this couple began to see the negative effects of her rebounding relationship with her parents. Good marriages must begin with individuals making a decisive separation from their parents. While I am not discouraging having a close and loving relationship with them, parents should not be used as an escape hatch when conflicts arise in the new home. There is a significant potential for abuse from too much parental involvement in a couple's marital problems.

2. Building togetherness and creating harmony. Wallerstein's second task involves putting together a shared vision of the future life together. "Building the new shared identity requires a shift from the 'I' of the emancipated adolescent and young adult to a solid and lasting 'we.' At the same time, the sense of we-ness has to include room for the autonomy of each partner."[4]

In marriage, all of a sudden, a new entity is formed. We can no longer think exclusively about what is best for "me"; we must plan for what is best for "us" in the years ahead. This requires a fundamental shift in our thinking. We no longer focus on advancing our own separate goals and interests but must look to our spouse as we develop mutually satisfying directions.

3. Becoming parents. For most couples, having children is a highpoint in their relationship. After children are born, many couples feel anchored in their marriage. Children are a miraculous gift from God, and it is no wonder that the marriage changes, usually for the better. God designed the family, and children are a natural part of His created order. They bring excitement, frustration, anger, joy, and a beloved chaos at times. But they typically stabilize the partners.

My wife and I are now empty-nesters, and it has not been an easy transition for us. While we certainly

Partnering Point

When a marriage matures, you can tolerate differences in each other. If she's social and he's a couch potato, it's okay for her to go out socially and for him to be home watching the ball game. Each one is happy that the other is having a good time; and neither one resents the other.

That's generous love. Selfish love is when she drags him out or he keeps her home. But that's not really love: that's control. it takes generous love to survive the large and small events of a long relationship. It takes generous love to keep on listening to each other—and to learn from each other.[5]

have other activities to occupy our time, we miss the commotion that once filled our home. Our two sons could never save our marriage when it was in crisis, but they definitely added a quality of stability unavailable to us otherwise. We now face a new challenge: redefining who we are and how we will relate to one another in the future. "In a successful marriage both husband and wife are able to face their internal conflicts and make room for the child. But at the same time they do not allow the child to take over the marriage."[6]

4. Coping with crises. Wallerstein's fourth task involves learning skills for coping with each crisis. Long-lasting marriages didn't happen simply by luck. They happen because the partners use the tools that we are discussing.

Not long ago I worked with a couple who had struggled with their son's leukemia. It was a golden opportunity for them to play the "blame game" as many do, turning their sadness and hurt against each other. While this tragedy was enough to bring down many marriages, this couple prepared themselves for the stress that a serious health problem would place on their marriage. It was tempting, they told me, to turn their hurt onto their partner. They were also tempted to invest all of their time, money, and emotional resources in this cataclysmic event to the exclusion of the rest of their family, and their marriage.

They decided they had to give all they could to their son, but it would not be helpful if they were always exhausted and their other children started to resent the extra attention given this son. Thus, they sought a balance between attending to the son's urgent needs, and also caring for themselves, their family, and their marriage.

5. Making a safe place for conflict. Wallerstein's fifth task, reiterating skills taught in this book, involves creating a safe environment where differences can be tolerated and even appreciated. "Conflict goes with the territory of marriage. Happy and unhappy marriages alike face the same demons, but in a poor marriage they tear at the fabric of the relationship and may destroy it. In a good marriage the demons are carefully contained."[7]

Dr. Wallerstein's experience fits my own as a psychologist. Couples in trouble tend to bicker and resent one another for having a difference of opinion. After a while, the layers of conflict are so great that the love is virtually buried, inaccessible to both. Caustic accusations ring out and four-letter words get thrown into the fray. This violates the security of the relationship, making it no longer safe to voice conflicting feelings and attitudes.

Couples who make a safe place for conflict realize that disagreement is simply part of any intimate relationship. We fight more with our spouses because we feel a sense of freedom without the customary pretenses. In lasting marriages, however, mates separate the meaty issues from nonissues. They choose their battles carefully. They let the other partner be genuine without demanding that he or she mold to a predetermined image. This freedom to be oneself creates a powerful bond in marriage.

6. Exploring sexual love and intimacy. Dr. Wallerstein suggests that the sixth task for the steadfast couple is to develop and maintain a vibrant sexual relationship. There is no better antidote to the pressures of living than a loving sex life.

This counsel is consistent with the Scriptures. God created man, but didn't stop there! He then became even more creative, got out some fresh tubes of paint, and created woman to be his helpmate—read "lover." Adam and Eve were commanded to subdue the earth and be fruitful and multiply. While most of us have a hang-up or two in this area, we shouldn't blame God for them. Repeatedly He counsels us to enjoy creation, and that includes our spouses.

But a certain pattern emerges in many marriages that are having difficulties in this area. The scenario goes like this:

Mr. Biggs works hard at his job. His work is an extension of who he is, and he is proud of how hard he works. He expects, as a token of the respect due him for his hard labor, to be rewarded sexually. He believes this should have little to do with the status of his relationship with his spouse. He is entitled to sex, regardless of how loving—*as she defines it!*—he is in return. He is entitled to sex regardless of whether or not their relationship is filled with conflict. It matters little to him that they have been fighting for the last three days. If he's in the mood, then he expects things to happen. In short, sex is something he *deserves*, separate from the love the couple has displayed toward one another.

So . . . he wants sex and will make her life miserable if he does not get it. And he has an entire arsenal of weapons to draw upon. For instance, he may threaten to get "it" elsewhere if he cannot get "it" at home. Sex, and his wife by extension, becomes an object to be obtained, as opposed to simply one part of a loving partnership.

I doubt that I need to tell you how all of this works for Mrs. Biggs. She has tried to tell him that sex is supposed to be a loving act between two people that flows from a caring and giving attitude. It occurs for her most naturally when both express their affection all the time. It happens most naturally when she feels cared for by

Strategy Steps
Contract Together!

If the Biggs' were to actually make a give-and-take transaction, how might it look? Here's a possible contract that could meet the needs of both partners:

If he will:

- Offer to help with the childcare and daily chores around the house;
- Assist her in feeling secure about the financial side of the relationship;
- Show affection and frequently touch her in nonsexual ways, without *always* expecting it to lead to sex;
- Tell her—and demonstrate—that he respects her and believes in her abilities;
- Communicate with her by talking and listening with undistracted focus;
- And, finally, create opportunities for romance and excitement . . .

Then, she will, in return:

- Show that she cares about him in return;
- Treat him with affection and respect;
- Be open to a vibrant sexual relationship as it flows within the context of relational and spiritual harmony.

his selfless giving in many small ways all day long. Kevin Leman's aptly titled *Sex Begins in the Kitchen* explains that sex actually begins at the beginning of the day, with the attitudes revealed over the morning cup of coffee. It rarely happens as an instant turn on, though that can be nice at times. Most importantly, it is not something that just happens in the *absence* of other affectionate activities.

Along these lines, Mrs. Biggs has some words of wisdom for her husband that could prove helpful to many men. She does not want to have a power struggle over how often they have sex. Nor is it her desire to withhold sex in order to drive him crazy, as he often suggests. It's not a manipulative attempt on her part to control him, as he often believes. The rules are simple, she suggests. The formula is easy; it's a transaction of *give and take—not just take*.

Many women are surprised at how much of a mystery developing an affectionate, sexual relationship seems to be for most men. It's as if they're thinking with some other part of their anatomy than their brains! Women want a healthy, alive sexual relationship too; however, they are often carrying more and more responsibilities and are not as able as men to simply block those responsibilities out of their minds.

They also need sex to be within the context of a caring and affectionate relationship that occurs throughout the day. If this will occur, they will usually be excited about sexual activities when the time is right.

7. Sharing laughter and keeping interest alive. As you navigate the river of healthy relating, are you recognizing some familiar territory? The tasks that we are exploring are, in many ways, similar to remedies promoted earlier in this book. I find this fact reassuring, because it suggests that there really are a limited number of skills to achieving a successful marriage.

This particular task recalls the previous discussion about keeping the adventure alive and well. Wallerstein says, "Although raising a family and making a living are serious pursuits, marriage has an equally serious purpose in providing an arena for play, humor, and lively interests. Just as a sexual relationship can become stale and lose its spontaneous passion, so too can a marriage become frozen into a dull repetition of daily routines. The nemesis of a good marriage is monotony unrelieved by imagination."[8] Wallerstein goes on to say that teasing, flirtation, and laughter, while they hint at insecurity, also banish tedium in a marriage. Humor has always been a way to keep the small annoyances in perspective.

8. Providing emotional nurturance. It should come as no surprise that we all still need emotional nurturance. Studies have long indicated that having dependable emotional support in our lives will help us be happier, healthier, and experience less stress. We desperately need someone with whom we can be totally honest. In this safe arena we are free to share our anxieties and frustrations and be comforted and understood. To be understood has been called the highest form of love.

It is interesting to watch youngsters who venture forth from their parents to explore the world. They constantly make their way back for refueling. Adults are not all that different. Setting off from home, we venture off to our stress-filled jobs, hectic schedules, demanding responsibilities, and yet need a haven where we can come to relax and safely whine just a little. We need a word of encouragement from someone who will comfort and reassure us that things will be okay.

9. *Preserving a double vision.* No, this is not an optometric problem! It is really a challenge to maintain, simultaneously, a vision of past memories and present realities. "Happily married couples treasure these images and episodes. The story of how they met and courted is given special status and dignity, set apart from everyone else's history."[10] We are challenged to "hold on to those idealized images of courtship and early history along with a realistic view of the present,

> # Strategy Steps
> ### Meeting Intimacy Needs of the Moment
>
> Caring involvement includes being with your spouse during high moments and low moments. It is at those moments that God wants to involve you in meeting your wife's or husband's intimacy needs. Paul the Apostle talks about offering words of "edification according to the need of the moment, so that it will give grace to those who hear it" (see Ephesians 4:29).
>
> **For example:**
>
> • at a moment of *loss*—your spouse needs to experience comfort through you,
>
> • at a moment of *failure*—your spouse needs to experience acceptance through you,
>
> • at a moment of *struggle*—your spouse needs to experience support through you.
>
> ***You are God's instrument of grace to meet the need of the moment!***[9]

including the changes wrought by time." Holding on to those memories not only binds our hearts together but also seems to buffer us from the inevitable disappointments that will occur along the way.

See Dick and Jane —*and You!*—Grow Up

I hope you have come to see that there is a Dick and Jane in all of us who can't wait to grow up. Yet our inherent childlikeness—which must never die out completely if we are to retain a God-given playfulness and wonder in life—resists all the changes that must occur if we're to be fully functioning adults. The challenges and tasks are great, but the rewards are greater. God has given us the ability to make the changes that we cannot make in our own strength.

So I encourage you, dear friend, to set your sights upon a lofty goal. Dare to believe that you can have a romantic, zesty relationship with your spouse. You want a vibrant marriage, so be willing to move beyond childish attitudes and behaviors. By committing yourself to the skills presented here, and to one another, you will arrive at a destination that is at once sacred and utterly exciting. Because you now have a purpose, plus the determination, you can move in the same direction with focus.

I would like to encourage you to approach the tasks, one step at a time. Go back through the Marriage Makeover plans with your spouse. Review your work regularly. Refocus on any chapter that seems to fit your most urgent situation. Blessings as you seek to improve your marriage and your life!

Think and Discuss

Consider the idea that "What gets your attention gets you." What currently has your attention? How has it created any imbalances in your life?

2. Marriage requires, at the least, goodwill, motivation, education, focus, perseverance, and humility. Consider each of those traits. Which are operating in your life, and which need more attention?

3. Picture your marriage as a God-given tool for transformation. How can your spouse help you become a mature individual—emotionally and spiritually?

4. Review the list of "marital anchors." Which have been set in your marriage?

5. Consider the most helpful principle for marital growth that you've learned from this book. How will you apply it in your life?

End Notes

Chapter 1

1. Doris Helmering, *Happily Ever After: A Therapist's Guide to Taking the Fight Out and Putting the Fun Back into Your Marriage* (New York: Warner Books, 1986), p. 86.

2. Dean Ornish, *Love and Survival* (New York: HarperCollins Publishers, 1998), p. 12.

3. David and Teresa Ferguson, *More Than Married* (Nashville: J. Countryman, 2000), p.34.

4. Chris Thurman, in *Today's Better Life*, Summer 1992, p. 41.

Chapter 2

1. M. Scott Peck, *People of the Lie* (New York: Simon and Schuster, 1997), pp. 77-78.

2. Adapted from David and Teresa Ferguson, *More Than Married* (Nashville: J. Countryman, 2000), p. 17-18.

3. Adapted from Joe Biuso and Brian Newman, *Receiving Love* (Colorado Springs: ChariotVictor Books, 1996), pp. 173-174.

4.Adapted from William Coleman, *Keeping Your Marriage from Burning Out* (San Bernardino, CA: Here's Life Publishers, 1989), p. 166.

Chapter 3

1. William Coleman, *Keeping Your Marriage from Burning Out* (San Bernardino, CA: Here's Life Publishers, 1989), p. 161.

2. Adapted from Kevin Leman, *Becoming a Couple of Promise* (Colorado Springs: NavPress, 1999), p. 85-87. Used by permission of NavPress (www.navpress.com or 800-366-7788). All rights reserved.

3. Robert Fulgham, *Everything I Really Need to Know I Learned in Kindergarten* (New York: Random House, 1993), pp. 174-175.

4. Adapted from David and Teresa Ferguson, *More Than Married* (Nashville: J. Countryman, 2000), pp. 72 and 85.

5. Adapted from Gary Smalley, *Secrets to Lasting Love* (New York: Simon and Schuster, 2000), p. 156-157.

Chapter 4

1. David and Teresa Ferguson, *More Than Married* (Nashville: J. Countryman, 2000), p. 11-12.

2. *Fast Company*, October, 1998, p. 110.

3. Adapted from Mira Kirshenbaum, *Too Good to Leave, Too Bad to Stay* (New York: Dutton, 1996), p. 245-246.

4. Charles Whitfield, *Co-dependence: Healing the Human Condition* (Deerfield Beach, FL: Health Communications, Inc., 1991), pp. 3-4.

5. Adapted from Part I of a self-test found in Frank Minirth, et. al., *The Complete Life Encyclopedia* (Nashville: Thomas Nelson Publishers, 1995), pp. 141-142.

Chapter 5

1. Adapted from Antoinette Saunders and Bonnie Remsberg, *The Stress-Proof Child* (New .York: Holt, Rinehart and Winston, 1984), pp. 129-130.

2. Adapted from Bonnie Maslin, *The Angry Marriage* (New York: Hyperion, 1994), np.

3. Gary Smalley, *Secrets to Lasting Love* (New York: Simon and Schuster, 2000), pp. 82-83.

4. Adapted from William Coleman, *Keeping Your Marriage from Burning Out* (San Bernardino, CA: Here's Life Publishers, 1989), p. 132.

5. Adrian Van Kaam, *The Dynamics of Spiritual Self-Direction*, (Denville, New Jersey: Dimension Books, 1976), np.

6. Adapted from Bill and Pam Farrel, *Love to Love You* (Eugene, OR: Harvest House Publishers, 1997), p. 50.

Chapter 6

1. Psychotherapy and a Christian View of Man, p. 134-135.

2. Henri Nouwen, "Forgiveness: The Name of Love in a Wounded World," *Weavings*, March/April, 1992, p. 10.

3. Henri Nouwen, p. 13.

4. Malcolm France, *The Paradox of Guilt* (London: Hoddertstoughton, 1967), pp. 19-20.

5. J. Vernon McGee, *Matthew*, (Pasadena, CA: Thru the Bible Books), 1973.

6. David Augsburger, *Caring Enough to Forgive* (Glendale, CA: Regal Books), 1981.

7. Lewis B. Smedes, *Forgive and Forget* (New York: Simon and Schuster, Inc.), 1984.

8. Bill and Pam Farrel, *Love to Love You* (Eugene, OR: Harvest House Publishers), 1997, p. 109-110.

Chapter 7

1. Kevin Leman, *Becoming a Couple of Promise* (Colorado Springs: NavPress), 1999, p. 46.

2. Doris Helmering, *Happily Ever After: A Therapist's Guide to Taking the Fight Out and Putting the Fun Back into Your Marriage* (New York: Warner Books, 1986), p. 160-161.

Chapter 8

1. Adapted from William Coleman, *Keeping Your Marriage from Burning Out* (San Bernardino, CA: Here's Life Publishers, 1989), p. 59-61.

2. Frank Minirth, Brian Newman, Robert Hemfelt, et. al., *Passages of Marriage* (Nashville: Thomas Nelson Publishers, 1991).

3. Judith Wallerstein and Sandra Blakeslee, *The Good Marriage*, (New York: Houghton Mifflin),1995. Excerpts reprinted by permission of Ticknor & Fields/Houghton Mifflin Co. All rights reserved.

4. Wallerstein, p. 62.

5. Daniel Gottlieb, quoted in Points to Ponder, Reader's Digest, Dec. '91.

6. Wallerstein, p.77

7. Wallerstein, p. 144.

8. Wallerstein, p. 202.

9. David and Teresa Ferguson, *More Than Married* (Nashville: J. Countryman), 2000, p.10.

10. Wallerstein, p. 323.

A Personal Note From the *Author*

Heart:

No matter where we are in our lives, there is always something that is not quite right. We feel troubled about our marriage, or relationship with our children, or perhaps are struggling with some challenging habit pattern. It is reassuring to know that we can trust God in all of our trials. Nothing touches us that has not touched Him first. He allows the sorrows of this world to touch us to keep us reliant upon Him, and remind us that He is all-sufficient for us. We must remember to "Consider it pure joy whenever you face trials of many kinds, because you know that the testing of your faith produces perseverance." (James 1:2)

Soul:

"For I know the plans I have for you, declares the Lord. Plans to prosper you and not to harm you. Plans to give you a hope and a future." (Jeremiah 29:11)

Lord, I pray for every reader and their struggles in this life. May they come to know your heart of love toward them, and learn to trust you no matter what comes their way.

Mind:

When I need nourishment for my spirit, apart from His Word, I often turn to the writings of Sue Monk Kidd. Her book, "When The Heart Waits: Spiritual Direction for Life's Sacred Questions" is especially personal to me. She helps me wait for answers in my impatience. I also like to read Henri Nouwen. His writings are so essential and refreshing to my spirit. A.W. Tozer reminds me of my need to have a deep love relationship with our Lord. I refer the reader to my web site for further encouragement at www.InCourageMinistry.com.

Strength:

I have heard it said that our passions are not created, they are discovered. Within each of us is a passion to make a difference during our temporary sojourn on this Earth. While here I encourage you to listen to the deepest yearnings in your heart; hold them before the Lord and seek ways to express them. Ponder them; muse about them; pray them. These are ways of discovering your truest self, and being that person God has created.

May God richly bless each one that reads this book, and may the eyes of your heart be enlightened.

Dr. David B. Hawkins